Start Your Own

EVENT PLANNING BUSINESS

Additional titles in *Entrepreneur's* Startup Series

Start Your Own

Arts and Crafts Business

Automobile Detailing Business

Bar and Club

Bed and Breakfast

Blogging Business

Business of eBay

Business Support Service

Car Wash

Child-Care Service

Cleaning Service

Clothing Store and More

Coaching Business

Coin-Operated Laundry

Construction and Contracting Business

Consulting Business

Crafts Business

Day Spa and More

e-Business

e-Learning Business

Event Planning Business

Executive Recruiting Business

Fashion Accessories Business

Florist Shop and Other Floral Businesses

Food Truck Business

Freelance Writing Business and More

Freight Brokerage Business

Gift Basket Service

Grant-Writing Business

Graphic Design Business

Green Business

Growing and Selling Herbs and Herbal Products

Hair Salon and Day Spa

Home Inspection Service

Import/Export Business

Information Consultant Business

Information Marketing Business

Kid-Focused Business

Mail Order Business

Medical Claims Billing Service

Net Services Business

Online Education Business

Personal Concierge Service

Personal Training Business

Pet Business and More

Pet-Sitting Business and More

Photography Business

Public Relations Business

Restaurant and More

Retail Business and More

Self-Publishing Business

Seminar Production Business

Senior Services Business

Specialty Travel and Tour Business

Staffing Service

Tutoring and Test Prep Business

Vending Business

Wedding Consultant Business

Wholesale Distribution Business

Entrepreneur
MAGAZINE'S

startup

3RD EDITION

Start Your Own

EVENT PLANNING BUSINESS

*Your Step-by-Step
Guide to Success*

Entrepreneur Press and Cheryl Kimball

EP
Entrepreneur
Press

Jere L. Calmes, Publisher
Cover Design: Beth Hansen-Winter
Production and Composition: Eliot House Productions

Library of Congress Cataloging-in-Publication Data
    Start your own event planning business/by Entrepreneur Press and Cheryl Kimball.—3rd ed.
      p.   cm.
    Previous ed. of this work by Entrepreneur Press and Amy Jean Peters.
    Includes index.
    ISBN-13: 978-1-59918-415-9 (alk. paper)
    ISBN-10: 1-59918-415-X (alk. paper)
      1. Special events—Planning. 2. Business planning. 3. Entrepreneurship. I. Kimball, Cheryl. II. Entrepreneur Press.
    GT3405.S73 2011
    394.2068—dc23   2011015171

Printed in the United States of America

15 14 13

10 9 8 7 6 5 4 3

Contents

Preface xi

Chapter 1
The Event Planning Industry 1
The Who, What, When, Where, and
    Why of Event Planning 2
    What Is Event Planning? .2
    When Do Event Planners Work? 3
    Where Do Event Planners Work? 4
    Why Do People Hire Event Planners? 4
    Who Becomes an Event Planner? 4
How Do Event Planners Do It? 8
A History Lesson 8
A Sophisticated Turn 9
Who Hires Event Planners? .10
    The Corporate Market 10
    The Social Market 11
Conducting Market Research 11
    The Market Analysis 11
    Interview Prospective Clients 13
    Analyze the Competition 13

Chapter 2
Building Your Business Foundation 15
Industry Research 16
Finding Your Niche 17
    Choosing a Specialty 18
Calculating Startup Costs 19
Creating a Map for Success 21
    Your Business Plan 21
    The Components of a Successful Business Plan 22
Crafting a Mission Statement 24

Chapter 3
A Day in the Life 25
Research 26
Design Time 31
    Developing Design Ideas 31
    Elements of Style 32
    Selecting a Site 32
    Creating the Perfect Décor 33
    Food, Glorious Food 35
    That's Entertainment 37
The Main Event 37
    All-Important Organization 38
    Organization Checklist 40
    Balancing the Logistics 40
Coordinating the Event 43
"You Cannot Rest on Your Laurels" 45

Chapter 4
Getting Started 49
It's All in a Name 50
Choosing a Business Location 53
Types of Business Forms 55
    Sole Proprietors 55
    General Partnership 56
    Limited Liability Company 56
    Corporations 56
Licenses and Permits 57
Choosing Insurance 59

Creating Effective Proposals
and Agreements 60
    Proposals 60
    Agreements 61

Chapter 5
Financing Your Business **69**
    The First Step 70
    Finding Financing 71
    Buying Equipment and Inventory. 73
        Essential Equipment 73
        Tracking Inventory 78

Chapter 6
Hiring Employees and Outside Vendors. **81**
    Reaching Out to Candidates. 84
    Advertising. 84
    Interviewing Applicants. 85
        Interviewing Strategies 85
    Paying Your Employees. 86
        Training Time 87
    Choosing Vendors 87
        Types of Vendors. 87
    Finding the A-List Suppliers. 88
        Negotiating with Vendors. 90
    Hiring Professional Help 91

Chapter 7
Marketing Your Business. **95**
    Networking to Business Success. 96
    The Ins and Outs of Advertising 97
    Your Business Card—Small but Mighty. 98
    The Informative Brochure 99
    Direct Mail. 100
    Newsletters 100
    Press Releases 100
    The Power of Customer Service. 101
    Giving Back to Your Community 102
    Building Your Image 103

▲

Chapter 8

Website Essentials...105

Setting Up a Website.................................. 106

Website Must-Haves.............................. 107

Your Homepage 108

Drilling Down................................... 109

The Rest of the Site 109

Contacting You from a Website 110

Trades.. 110

Marketing Your Website 111

Your Website URL 112

Keep 'Em Interested 112

Choosing a Web Host................................. 113

Chapter 9

The World of Social Media 115

Traditional Media with a Digital Twist.................. 116

E-Newsletters 116

Press Releases 117

Social Media.. 118

Blogs 119

Facebook 120

LinkedIn 121

Twitter 121

Chapter 10

Managing Your Finances.............................. 123

Financial Statements 124

Paying Your Vendors 125

Pricing Your Services................................ 125

Maintaining Cash Flow 128

Adding Up the Costs for an Event...................... 129

Calculating When Your Business Will Break Even........ 131

You and Your Taxes 132

Deducting Expenses 134

Chapter 11

Planner Profiles 137

Wedding Planner.................................... 138

Fundraising Planners. 140
Corporate Planners 141
Educational Planners. 142
Other Event Planners 142
   Music Planners 143
   Major Milestones Planners. 143
   Graduations, Homecomings, and More 143
Profiles. 144
   Amy Piper, Signature Events 144
   Cheryl Hagner, Wesleyan University. 145
   Kym Nason, Nonprofit Fundraiser 146
   Erin Kelley, Stargazer Events. 147
   Scott Marshall, Seacoast Events 148

Chapter 12
Onward and Upward **149**
   Keep Your Business Healthy. 150
   When Bad Things Happen
   to Good Event Planners 152
   Recipe for Success 153
   Looking Ahead. 155

Appendix
Event Planning Resources **157**
   Associations 157
   Books 158
   Educational Opportunities 159
   Event Planning Software. 159
   Industry Experts 159
   Magazines and Publications 160
   Websites of Interest to Event Planners 160
   Successful Event Planners. 161

Glossary **163**

Index **167**

Preface

At the time the first edition of *Start Your Own Event Planning Business* was printed in 2004, event planning had taken a bit of a downturn as the country was still reeling from 9/11 and getting back on track after a few years of a less than robust economy. Between that first printing and the time the second edition came out in 2007, the field of event planning blossomed. A leading business magazine back then described event planning as one of the nation's "top jobs," ranking this fast-paced and energized career at Number 39. This same analysis predicted double-digit growth for the field.

And then we all know what happened. The economy tanked. Companies started holding back on corporate functions, meetings, and travel in general. Even brides and grooms, notoriously blissfully unaware of things like budgets, started to negotiate deals and ask for cost efficiencies.

But as this new edition of *Start Your Own Event Planning Business* goes to press, things are looking up for the event planning industry. Companies are getting back on track and as companies thrive, they turn to event planners to hold myriad events every year. Brides and grooms are getting back to their "anything goes for our special day" attitudes. In fact, the U.S. Bureau of Labor Statistics expects a 16 percent growth in the event planning job outlook over the next seven years.

Growth in the event planning industry also owes thanks to globalization. As companies create and develop global imprints with employees located at offices circling the earth, these businesses must periodically gather their employees for meetings and conferences. As globalization continues to expand, the demand for event planners to create and manage these global retreats will increase. Even teleconferences require someone to organize them for effectiveness.

There also has been substantial growth in the number of events held by government agencies. Much of this growth has been spurred by post-9/11 response, focusing on bolstering homeland security.

Baby boomers are doing their part, too, increasing the demand for event planners. As the boomers age, they are holding ever more elaborate birthday parties and anniversaries, all of which are orchestrated by savvy event planners.

Event planning is a field that offers a wide array of career possibilities. Several of the planners interviewed for this book started their planning businesses on a part-time basis while they focused on a young family. Others have planned hundreds of events and some even do it full time as an employee.

These varied models are another factor in the increasing attractiveness of the event-planning field. The field can accommodate anybody—from part- to full-time—who has the enthusiasm for developing a business in this ever-changing, always exciting business area.

1

The Event Planning Industry

This book is a guide to developing a thriving business in this rapidly growing industry. It is an exciting time to throw your party hat into the event planning ring, as event planners are being called upon to develop and stage literally millions of events every year. These events range from first-birthday parties to political fundraisers, anniversaries, bar and bat mitzvahs, fashion shows, product launches, conferences, graduations, and reunions, to name just a few!

According to a recent report in *The Wall Street Journal*, it takes about 150 hours for a planner, working with her staff, to produce a major event from start to finish. You do the math. Millions of events multiplied by 100s of hours spent planning equals many, many opportunities for those entering this field.

> ## Smart Tip — Tip...
> If you are planning an event in a foreign country, do your research! Little things can be big headaches. For example, *Meetings & Conventions* reports that Europe and other overseas locations no longer accept credit cards with the magnetic strip. Savvy planners will be ahead of the curve on these kinds of details.

Yes, working in the field of event planning can mean long hours and high-stress moments—when the kitchen is accidentally set ablaze, for instance (something that Cheryl Hagner, Director of University Events and Scheduling at Wesleyan University, faced with aplomb). For the event planners interviewed in this guide, though, the rewards far outweigh any possible negatives. The field of event planning is fast-paced, creative, innovative, energizing, and offers the real possibility for earning big dollars.

This first chapter offers an overview, looking at what event planners do and why they do it. The chapter also includes an overview of the special events industry and a sampling of ideas for conducting your own market research, a must-do when creating a new business of any kind.

The Who, What, When, Where, and Why of Event Planning

We begin by considering the who, what, when, where, why, and how of event planning (although not in that order).

What Is Event Planning?

This question actually breaks down into two questions: What kinds of events are we talking about? What is event planning?

First, what kinds of events are we talking about? They include:

- Celebrations (fairs, parades, weddings, reunions, birthdays, anniversaries, bar and bat mitzvahs, first communions, Sweet 16s)

- Education (conferences, conventions, meetings, graduations)
- Promotions (product launches, political rallies, fashion shows, conventions)
- Commemorations (memorials, civic events)

The above list is not an exhaustive one, but as the examples illustrate, special events may be business related, purely social, or somewhere in between. The advice in this book is relevant to the planning of both business and social events.

Now we move to the second What question: What is event planning?

Planners of an event may handle any or all of the following tasks related to that event:

- Conduct research
- Create an event design
- Find a site
- Arrange for food, decor, and entertainment
- Plan transportation to and from the event
- Send invitations to attendees
- Arrange any necessary accommodations for attendees
- Coordinate the activities of event personnel
- Hire employees to work the event
- Supervise at the site
- Conduct evaluations of the event

How many of these activities your business engages in will depend on the size and type of a particular event, which will, in turn, depend on the specialization you choose. Your specialization will, of course, depend on your areas of expertise, but also will depend on your location. If you live in rural Iowa, for instance, you may be planning to develop a social event planning business since you may not have a strong corporate presence in your town.

When Do Event Planners Work?

Few event planners, if any, have 9-to-5 jobs (unless, of course, they have a day job and conduct their event planning as a sideline; this strategy may be a good one if you are just starting out). By its very nature, event planning tends to involve evenings, weekends, holidays, and sometimes even specific seasons. How much time, and when, you must commit to working will depend, once again, on the specialization you choose.

Industry expert John Daly (www.jdalyinc.com) points out that summer is a slow period for corporate events. Also, by the second week in December, all the corporate holiday events are over.

As a general rule, social events involve more weekends and holidays than corporate events. Some areas of the country and some types of events have on and off seasons. However, no matter what your specialization (with the exception of parties for young children), you can count on working at least some evenings as you coordinate and supervise events. The planning of those events, however, will be done mostly during business hours.

> **Smart Tip** Tip...
>
> It is vital that you consider your life and lifestyle as you plan a business in event planning. If you are raising young children, for instance, be sure that you have a system in place for reliable child care. Nothing will sink your business faster than if you are forced to miss events because your babysitter didn't show up as planned.

Where Do Event Planners Work?

Some event planners work out of their homes, while others rent office space for their businesses. Each of these strategies has advantages and disadvantages. Chapter 4 offers more advice on choosing the ideal location for your business.

Why Do People Hire Event Planners?

This question has a simple answer: Often individuals find that they lack the expertise and the time to plan events themselves. Independent planners can step in and give these events the attention they deserve.

Large businesses hire event planners to produce the myriad events—from golf tournaments to trade shows with tens of thousands of attendees—that are necessary each year.

People who make use of event planners also understand the connections that a planner brings to the process. And it can be a great advantage to have someone planning your event who has no personal vested interest in it.

Who Becomes an Event Planner?

Planners are often people who got their start in one particular aspect of special events.

Lauren Polastri, owner of The Other Woman, an event planning business based in Connecticut, laid the foundation for her business with a thriving catering business. Initially, Lee J. Howard Entertainment Inc. in Atlanta (www.leejhowardentertainment. com) provided entertainment only. Then, in response to client requests, Howard branched out. Many other planners have similar stories. This explains why planners often not only coordinate entire events, but also may, in addition, provide one or more services for those events.

Often, owners of event planning businesses are also people who planned events for other companies before deciding to go into business for themselves. New York City planner Jaclyn Bernstein planned events for another company before she and partner Robert Hulsmeyer bought it and turned it into Empire Force Events Inc. (www.empireforce.com).

Although the backgrounds of event planners may vary greatly, planners share many traits. Everyone we interviewed insisted that you have to have a passion for the event planning industry. Many said that they can't wait to get to the office most days. As industry expert Dr. Joe Goldblatt notes, "Successful event managers love their jobs."

John Daly, floral design specialist and industry expert, has written for industry publications, including *Special Events* magazine. He also does a lot of public speaking. When he is asked about profits in the industry, he replies, "You have to get the passion, then the money will come. It's hard work. But it's rewarding if it's your passion."

Many planners stressed that they didn't get into the event planning industry because they want to get rich, but because they have a passion for it. Not only is getting acknowledgment for a job well done powerful, but most successful event planners thrive on each new challenge.

Joyce Barnes-Wolff has had many clients give her this figurative pat on the head. When she planned her first event, her task involved ". . . putting on a pot of coffee and calling the press and trying to get 25 people to show up." She learned and grew along with the retail company she worked for, and her last event for that company was a shareholders meeting for 18,000 people. After that, she planned events for a production company for about five years before starting her own business, JBW Productions (www. jbwproductions.com). Although her company is

Smart Tip

Golf outings took a hit during the economic downturn, but these events are, and should be according to reports in *Meetings & Conventions*, a mainstay of the corporate event repertoire. Golfing provides a unique environment for chatting it up with clients and prospective clients. Tournaments can provide valuable contributions to charitable causes and get companies into the visibility of new customers.

Profile

Cheryl Hagner, Director of University Events and Scheduling at Wesleyan University, emphasizes the importance of good communication and truly listening to clients. "Don't push your agenda. You absolutely want your clients to be comfortable with the conclusion. When I first meet with a client, I say, 'Tell me what you want and we'll do it.'"

▲

Do You Have "The Right Stuff"?

Event planners and industry experts have plenty of philosophies about their field and about their own roles in event planning. "Goodwill matters a lot in this business," says industry expert John Daly. "It's important to share knowledge." His motto? "Big fun is serious business."

"In this industry there is no right or wrong except to make the client happy," says expert David Granger.

Planners design events, hire personnel, and also contribute their own labor where needed. Joyce Barnes-Wolff views creative work as a major contribution her company makes to events. But creativity, she cautions, is not everything. "Without planning and follow-through, it's like a roof without a foundation," she says.

When asked about the qualities of successful event planners, Lee J. Howard has these succinct words: "Grace under pressure."

Jaclyn Bernstein knows exactly why event planners stick it out through pressure, crazy hours, and deadlines. "You have to love what you're doing," she says.

And, you may ask, what about a shared, industrywide philosophy? Is there a motto? You bet. "You're only as good as your last event."

now seven years old, she did not initially intend to strike out on her own. "I was handed a chunk of business," she says. Her local convention visitors bureau hired her directly to produce the Capitol Lights event. Since she began her business, her company has expanded to produce other corporate and nonprofit events.

What about the personality of event planners? When asked what traits are important in the industry, planners listed the following:

- *Organizational ability.* Everyone mentioned this trait. Therefore, be warned: If you would rather count every blade of grass on your lawn than make a list, this profession is not for you.

- *Attention to detail.* This is another must mentioned by most interviewees. Planners must think of, and keep track of, an amazing number of details. Planner Lee J. Howard suggests the following strategy: "Think from the completion of the result you want and then work backward to see how you can get there."

- *A stout heart.* You can't be faint-hearted and be a successful planner. You are in charge of the entire event, and there are no second chances.

- *Nerves of steel.* Glitches or no glitches, you must be upbeat and positive during the event. (You can cry and gnash your teeth later, in the car.)

- *Decision-making ability.* Anyone who is always the last of a group to order at a restaurant should consider a different industry. As an event planner, you will be called upon to make many decisions, sometimes in only a split second.

- *Good communication skills.* You'll need to convey your ideas and plans effectively to your clients, staff, and vendors, among others. You will need this ability not only as a sender, but also as a receiver of communication. Keep in mind that communication can be visual as well as verbal. Recognizing a blank look when you see one can enable you to clarify directions before some aspect of the event goes awry.

- *A liking for people.* This industry is very people-oriented. Jaclyn Bernstein mentioned a propensity for "taking care of people."

- *Creativity.* Whether you handle design elements of an event or not, creative talents are a definite plus. Furthermore, the definition of creativity may not always be what you think. "Creative is when you're on the job and Plan A isn't going to work and you have half an hour to figure out Plan B," says Patty Sachs, author of *Pick a Party Cookbook: The Big Book of Theme Party Refreshments and Table Décor,* among other books.

- *Flexibility.* To be able to think on your feet and be ready to change from your plan is key, since something—sometimes a tiny thing, sometimes a big thing—will go differently from even the most carefully constructed plan.

- *Tact.* Sometimes you will have to break unhappy news to clients. For example, their budgets may not always be big enough to accomplish what they want. Also, they may want décor elements that either will not work well or are inappropriate. While these problems are less common when dealing with corporate clients, you will still find tact a necessary ingredient in successful business relationships.

If you have most of these traits, event planning may be a good profession for you. How do you find out for sure? "Volunteer, volunteer, volunteer!" says Sachs. "Offer to assist the chairperson of a large fundraising event, the bigger the better. Follow that person through from start to finish, sitting in on all meetings and pushing the event over the hill, grunt work included. This will establish the area of planning that you find most appealing and for which you are most suited." If you

Smart Tip

If you decide to volunteer, make sure you are not an "invisible" volunteer, one of the masses. Make sure you are assisting the person in charge and that you get experience with a large variety of tasks.

already have some idea of which types of events you'd like to plan, make sure you concentrate your volunteer efforts there.

How Do Event Planners Do It?

The answer to this question is what this book, as well as your own experience, will show you. So pull up a comfortable chair and read on. Our first step will be to examine the event planning industry itself.

Smart Tip

Depending on the type of services they offer, independent planners might call themselves by any of the following titles: program manager, project manager, event planner, principal executive, fundraising consultant, development consultant, meeting consultant, or event coordinator, among others.

A History Lesson

The special events industry has grown enormously in the last two decades. According to recent research conducted by Dr. Joe Goldblatt, Certified Special Events Professional (CSEP), annual spending for special events worldwide is estimated at $500 billion. Goldblatt is the founder of International Special Events Society (ISES) and the founding director of the Event Management Program at George Washington University. Currently at Johnson and Wales University, he is the dean of the Alan Shawn Feinstein Graduate School, which offers the first MBA concentration in Event Leadership.

According to U.S. government census information, job growth in this field is on the uptick. Globalization has added to this surge as these multinational businesses call on event planners to develop meetings for their globetrotting staffs. These companies recognize that only so much work can be conducted via phone and e-mail (remember the deals that are made on the golf course when business associates come face-to-face!). Ultimately, the players in these large corporations need to come together in one place. This is when the event planner is called into play.

Studies show that the average event planner now earns about $60,000, with plenty of room for growth to this already healthy income.

Goldblatt adds that the social events market is booming. "As the baby boomers age, they have more to celebrate—and do!" He points out that a record number of Americans are turning 50 in the next few years—and they will mark their birthdays with flashy events.

Sachs agrees, "The event, party, and celebration industry is growing more each year, in a steady way." Like Goldblatt, she points out the large number of baby boomers celebrating milestone birthdays. In addition, she says, many are now celebrating landmark anniversaries or their offsprings' graduations and weddings. "To top all of this, these baby boomers are often owners or executives in businesses that were established some 25 years ago, which brings about many corporate celebrations."

Also booming is the children's birthday party business, with over-the-top first birthday celebrations and extravagant Sweet 16s contributing to the rapid growth of this aspect of event planning.

Although potential profits, especially in social event planning, are substantial, keep in mind that it takes the average event planning

Bright Idea

When a company holds a meeting in a major city and the attendees travel to the meeting from other cities or states, a planner may use a destination manager's services to take care of the attendees' needs at their meeting location. Destination managers coordinate and supervise meetings in their cities, transport attendees to and from their hotels and airports, and take attendees on tours to give them a feel for the cities they are visiting. Jaclyn Bernstein, president of Empire Force Events Inc. in New York City, handles a lot of destination management business.

 business two to three years to make a healthy profit. Why? One reason is that most clients come from word-of-mouth referrals, and it can take a while before a solid base of contacts is developed. More about building a solid client base will be covered in Chapter 7.

A Sophisticated Turn

Along with increased demand for special events, and perhaps because of it, the industry has become much more sophisticated. According to industry expert Daly, "It's become a force to be reckoned with." Twenty years ago, he says, a party was a tablecloth and a centerpiece. Event planners were not taken seriously. When he told people he created parties for a living, he remembers, it was laughable. "Now it's interesting," he says.

David Granger, a veteran in the industry, concurs. "People know what they are looking for," he says. "A certain quality is expected now."

Joyce Barnes-Wolff makes a similar point: "There is more credibility than . . . when event specialists were the people who did country club parties." Now, she adds, huge concerns like Disney, Radio City Music Hall, Universal Studios, Paramount, and others have become involved in the special events industry.

▲

Who Hires Event Planners?

Broadly speaking, there are two markets for event planning services: corporate and social. Market information is more readily available for corporate meetings than for other events, but we will attempt to give you a good idea of both markets.

The Corporate Market

We will use the term corporate to include not only companies but also charities and nonprofit organizations. All these entities use special events to reach their target markets and to increase their visibility in the community. In fact, special events have become increasingly important as competition forces organizations to look for new ways to get their messages across to consumers or contributors.

Charities and nonprofit organizations host gala fundraisers, receptions, and athletic competitions, among other events, to expand their public support base and raise the funds they require. Such organizations find that special events are cost-effective and have a high impact. Thousands of these events occur each year, and although the large ones require specialized event planning experience, you may find smaller local events to plan.

Companies host trade shows, conventions, company picnics, holiday parties, and meetings for staff members, board members, or stockholders. There is a huge market for these types of events. In one year alone, the total number of meetings held in the United States is well above 1 million, according to the latest (2008) Meetings Market Report conducted for *Meetings & Conventions* magazine.

Whether you plan meetings, fundraisers, or receptions, there are opportunities available in corporate event planning.

Patty Sachs, author of party-planning books and newsletters, says that corporations want events that are original and striking enough to be long remembered: "Themes are extremely popular." Lauren Polastri, of The Other Woman, has also found that her clients are asking for more event-themed parties and events. Unusual sites, customized entertainment, and an increased degree of guest involvement are also gaining in popularity. The bottom line for most party givers—corporate or social—is that they want to feel that their party was special or unique in some way.

Planning corporate events can provide you with a steady, profitable amount of

Stat Fact
The Meetings Market Report is conducted every two years and published in *Meetings & Conventions* magazine, a leading source for the meetings industry.

business, but if you are a beginning event planner, Daly recommends that you begin by planning social events.

The Social Market

Social events include weddings, birthdays, anniversary parties, bar and bat mitzvahs, Sweet 16 parties, children's parties, reunions, etc. You may decide to handle all these events or to specialize in one or more of them.

Most people who employ event planners for these types of parties are in the middle- to upper-income levels and have some spare income but no spare time. Such clients are likely to live in affluent suburbs. Typically, these clients have household incomes of at least $60,000.

The market for social events, especially birthdays and anniversaries, is expected to continue to increase over the next few years, as baby boomers mature. This group has children getting married, parents celebrating golden anniversaries, and their own silver wedding anniversaries to celebrate. Industry experts agree that baby boomers will be a major source of income for event planning entrepreneurs in the coming years.

Conducting Market Research

Many interviewees told us that their market research was very informal in nature, consisting of knowledge gained through years of involvement in the industry. Deborah Williams, Kim Quigley, and David Granger all have years of experience in the event planning or supply industry. Their target market is the Dallas-Ft. Worth area. However, they also operate nationally, producing corporate events in Florida, Oklahoma, and Ohio. Most of their clients come to them through organizations they belong to or because they have been involved in the industry for many years. "So you know the resources and the people," Quigley says.

If you already have experience in event planning or a related industry, you may be starting your own business partly because discussions with colleagues make you aware that a need exists. This kind of knowledge is valuable, but Goldblatt points out that competition is now global as well as local, and all event planners should do market research. With this idea in mind, we now offer some suggestions on how to conduct this type of research.

The Market Analysis

One of your first tasks is to determine the market limits or trading area of your business. These limits will vary depending upon the type of event planning service you offer. For example, if you plan parties, you may limit your market to your county. If you plan corporate meetings, however, you may have a national client base.

Studies show that a population base of at least 50,000 is needed to support an event planning service. Keep in mind that the higher the income level of that population, the more potential clients there will be for your business.

If you live in an area with a population base of less than 50,000, consider your goals. Perhaps you are a mother of young children and are hoping to earn $5,000 a year, keeping your business small while rearing your children. Then a smaller population base may work for you. Many event planners put their hats into this business planning to earn only a part-time salary to supplement other family income. This is one of the real strengths of this field. You can choose to create a successful part-time or full-time business in event planning.

To conduct a market analysis you need to ask and answer the following questions:

- Is the population base large enough to support your event planning service?
- Does the community have a stable economic base that will provide a healthy environment for your business?
- Are the area's demographic characteristics compatible with the market you wish to serve?

Many chambers of commerce have offices that track their area's economic development. These offices are usually called either Office of Economic Development or Economic Development Council. Find an office in your area, and look for the above information. In addition, look at reports and studies conducted by trade associations. You can also contact the Census Bureau at www.census.gov.

You can also access www.bls.gov/cex/ to read the Bureau of Labor's Consumer Expenditure Survey. This survey includes information about how individuals and families spend their money.

If you'll be planning corporate events, you also need to know the number of corporations in your service area that hold regular conventions and meetings, the size of these companies, their budgets for these events, and if they are using outside services. You will be able to find answers to many of these questions on a company's website.

As you conduct your market research, memberships in industry-related associations can be well worth the investment. Associations usually offer networking opportunities and a wealth of industry-specific information, such as market statistics, member lists, books, and reference materials. They may also offer discounts on purchases from certain suppliers.

There are several associations specific to the event planning industry, including the International Special Events Society (ISES) and Meeting Professionals International

(MPI). For information on contacting an industry association, please see the Appendix at the end of this guide.

Interview Prospective Clients

The next step is to interview prospective clients. What are their needs? How likely are they to use a service like yours? If you are planning corporate events, interview meeting planners and directors of marketing and public relations, as well as event directors at convention halls and hotels. If your business will focus on social events, interview women in affluent households (studies show women do most social planning). Whatever your specialization, also consider interviewing professionals in related fields. Photographers and caterers know a lot about the nature of the special events occurring in the area. You can survey your targeted market by direct mail, by telephone, by e-mail, or in person.

Next, Goldblatt suggests, try to get a few clients. "If people are not willing to pay you, they're not fully committed," he says.

Analyze the Competition

Competition in the event planning market is fierce, but it is not insurmountable. If you are targeting the corporate market, your competition will consist not only of other event planning entrepreneurs, but also of in-house meeting planners hired by corporations. Many corporations choose to outsource event planning responsibilities to keep costs low. You may be able to assess the competition by asking corporations about the planners they work with. Trade associations such as ISES or MPI may not be able to disclose members' names, but they might be willing to tell you how many of their members are located in your area.

In the social arena, your main competition will be other event planning entrepreneurs, as well as some caterers, florists, etc., who have taken on the responsibilities of planning events as a sideline function. Most of the competition you'll face will be local; try checking in your phone book under Event Planners or Party Planners to see how many others there are. Be aware, however, that many event planners do not buy advertising, preferring to rely solely on word of mouth to do their advertising for them. This means you may have to get creative to figure out how much local

Dollar Stretcher

Check with area colleges and universities for free assistance in conducting your market research. Many schools will give credit to business students for helping you to do your market research. They receive college credit, you receive valuable information, and everyone is happy!

competition you face. Ask vendors which planners they work with. Go to party supply stores and see if you can find out who their major customers are. Ask all your questions face-to-face, rather than by phone. If you are friendly and explain that you are trying to figure out if there is enough demand for another planning business, most people will cooperate.

If you find a large amount of competition in your area, don't be discouraged. Instead, look for a niche you can fill and think about what will make your event planning company stand out in the crowd. Social event planning is the ideal place from which to launch your career. Social planning is a growth industry—there are more opportunities out there than those planners in the marketplace can handle. Social event planners also will be able to find plenty of work in areas with a smaller population base.

Remember that if you strive to be the best, research your market, promote yourself, and develop a good business plan, you will find your spot in the marketplace.

Building Your Business Foundation

Now that you've decided to pursue a career in event planning, it is time to build a solid foundation upon which to build your business. Before you plan your first event, you will need to research the industry, find your niche, determine startup costs, and create a plan for business success.

Industry Research

Some aspects of event planning are much more complicated than many entrepreneurs realize. The intricacies of developing solid vendor relations, establishing good rapport with clients, and heading off potential problems before they affect your event (and therefore your reputation) can only be conquered by study and experience.

Even so, your research shouldn't stop here. You should also do the following:

- Conduct the market research as outlined in Chapter 1. There is no substitute for doing your homework.

- Online research. The internet has become an invaluable tool for doing research. Not only do you have access to many trade journals, but you can also search other event planners and find out what they are doing, how they are marketing themselves, what their website looks like, and myriad other helpful details that you can pick and choose from to incorporate into your own plans.

Event Planning News

Event planners interviewed for this guide point out that the field of event planning has become increasingly complex, as consumer tastes become more sophisticated and more elaborate events are staged. Because of this growing complexity, it is becoming increasingly common for event planners to earn a bachelor's degree, according to U.S. Census information. Degrees in marketing, communications, and business are useful to event planners as they develop their businesses. Remember, though, a degree is not required, and, as event planners point out, degree or no degree, nothing beats real, in-the-trenches event planning experience.

- Network with other event planning entrepreneurs and business owners by joining local associations. Industry ties are crucial in the event planning business.

- Contact the national associations for the latest in research and practice guidelines, as well as for any other help they can provide. You can find the relevant contact information in the Appendix.

- Keep up with industry trends through business journals and other publications. These are valuable resources.

- Read everything you can find on the event planning industry. This includes newspaper features and articles in glossy magazines such as *Vanity Fair* and *Town & Country*, which chronicle the parties of the rich and powerful. Reading these glossies will help you to keep on top of trends, essential in this business.

- Volunteer your time to a local charity event. Not only will you get hands-on experience, but also you'll make valuable contacts that will help you down the road. Be an effective volunteer—not a wallflower. Make your presence known to the organizer of the event.

Finding Your Niche

We've already mentioned the fact that most event professionals focus on either corporate or social events. However, you should consider specializing even further, narrowing your attention to children's parties, corporate retreats, or other types of events. Why? "Without a niche market, it makes it hard for the market consumer to find you," says Dr. Joe Goldblatt, industry expert and founder of ISES. For example, if you're known as your community's expert on anniversary parties, a client wanting to throw such a party is more likely to come to you than to a general party planner.

Specializing in one or two types of events will also make your job easier. You can become an expert in one type of event faster than you can in multiple events. Specializing will save you time because you'll soon be familiar with all the elements of, and vendors required for, the type of event you choose. And as an event professional, time is one of your most valuable resources—the more you can save, the better.

Selecting a niche will also help you to save on startup costs since you will need to buy supplies only relevant to your specialization. For instance, if you choose children's

---

Making the Grade

Consider getting a degree or certificate from a local university in event planning or management. According to industry expert Dr. Joe Goldblatt, 300 colleges and universities offer classes in event management. A list of the institutions offering educational opportunities in this field is available from Meeting Professionals International (MPI). (See the Appendix for contact information.)

Also consider working to become a Certified Special Events Professional (CSEP) or Certified Meeting Planner (CMP). These designations are given out by International Special Events Society (ISES) and MPI, respectively. Many corporations, and some members of the general public, look for these designations when hiring planners. Because of the research and study it takes to become a CMP or CSEP, clients know that these planners are professionals.

[handwritten margin note: MPI list of schools]

birthday party planning as your niche, you won't need to buy complicated event-planning software designed for larger events.

Choosing a Specialty

Industry expert, consultant, and author Patty Sachs agrees that specializing is a good way to establish yourself in the industry. She suggests the following possible niches for social event planners:

- Weddings are perhaps the most focused and common event planning service provided
- Hospitality suites (events held in the "party" room of a retirement home or a business)
- Parties away from home (events hosted by hotel guests)
- Surprise parties
- Progressive parties (events at more than one venue, usually involving transportation from one location to another—e.g., tours, scavenger hunts)
- His 'n' hers showers (wedding and baby)
- Birthday parties for one-year-olds
- Theme parties
- "Golden" parties (50th anniversaries, 50th birthdays, etc.)
- Milestone birthdays
- Weekend event guest services (events to entertain out-of-town guests over the weekend—e.g., tours, barbecues)
- Kids' parties
- Kids' event areas for grown-up parties

The niches listed above all have a social focus, even though your client might also be a corporation. The following are some additional

Profile

Event planner David Granger, now with *Bravo!* Entertainment, got his start in event planning volunteering with the LA Marathon. Granger takes leadership and education in the industry seriously. He is currently a member of the Society of Talent and Entertainment Professionals (STEP) of Texas, a past president of the International Special Event Society, Dallas Chapter, a member of the Dallas Convention and Visitors Bureau, and is also involved with the Dallas Gay and Lesbian Chamber of Commerce and a member of the International Association of Corporate Entertainment Professionals (IACEP).

Bright Idea

Themed parties are always in style. Ideas are everywhere—seasonal themes, characters from kids' stories like Harry Potter, and regional parties, like a South of the Border flare that focuses on the colors and tastes associated with Mexico and South America are just a few examples.

possibilities for finding your niche in business-related events:

- Mall events (fashion shows, store grand openings, department-store promotions)
- Meetings and conferences
- Awards events
- Fundraisers
- Corporate retreats or picnics

If you do decide to focus on one type of event, be sure that your market area has enough of a demand, as discussed in Chapter 1. If you live in a rural area, developing a business based on organizing corporate meetings and conferences is probably not as sensible—or as profitable—as developing an event planning business focusing on social events.

Profile

Industry expert John Daly, CSEP, started his first event planning company in the mid-'70s on $4,000. He drove an old van, which he parked out of sight. His first location was a 250-square-foot workroom in Los Angeles. He spent the majority of his startup money on two suits. "I wanted to look successful," he explains. "It worked." Within four years he had 35 full-time employees and a fleet of cars. "I was at the right place at the right time."

Calculating Startup Costs

How much money will you need to start your event planning business? That will depend on the cost of living in the area your business serves and whether you work from home or rent office space. It will also depend on your own taste and lifestyle choices.

Keep in mind that while working from home will keep your costs low, you must still buy equipment and a good insurance policy. You may also need advertising, although many event planners rely solely on word-of-mouth advertising.

All these expenses can be costly. The Startup Expenses Worksheet on page 21 will help to give you an indication of how much money you will need to start your event planning service. Fill in the column labeled "My Own" with your own estimated costs.

This chart lists the startup costs for two hypothetical event planning services. The first business is homebased with no permanent employees. The owner already has a basic computer and modem and some office furniture. She used her startup money to buy liability insurance, event planning software, a better cell phone, a digital camera, and a multifunction printer/copier/fax machine. She also established a website and paid a graphic design student to produce a high-quality business card and letterhead logo. She started her business on a shoestring.

Special Delivery

Most planners we interviewed specialized in either social or corporate events, with little mixing of the two types. Which of these you choose (or whether you choose to mix them) will depend on several factors:

○ *Amount of experience.* Industry expert John Daly points out that corporations are extremely sophisticated. If you are just starting out in the industry, he recommends beginning with private events. "You have to get seasoned before you do corporate events."

○ *Personality.* Clients tend to have more invested, emotionally, in social events. Generally speaking, social event planning requires even greater degrees of patience and tact than does corporate event planning.

○ *Lifestyle preference.* Consider what you expect as time off and whether you have strong feelings about the time of year you'd like to vacation. Everyone interviewed mentioned that they work long hours, well above 40 per week. "Private parties take a lot more time than corporate events. They're much more demanding," says Daly. This is partly because of the client's emotional investment in the event. Working during holidays is a virtual certainty if you do social parties. Furthermore, specializing in wedding anniversary parties might have you heavily booked in the spring and gasping for work the rest of the year. Planning children's birthday parties will, in most cases, leave your evenings free. A corporate specialization, on the other hand, may involve more travel.

The higher end business occupies 1,000 square feet of office space. The owner/manager of this business employs a full-time junior planner and a part-time bookkeeper, as well as temporary employees who handle clerical work and who may help prepare for various events. This owner upgraded her existing computer equipment, bought office furniture and cell phones for herself and her assistant, added a phone line and a website, bought several types of insurance, and invested in business cards, stationery, and an ad in the Yellow Pages.

Both owners will derive their income from pre-tax net profit. Annually, these new businesses will gross $85,000 and $250,000, respectively. The startup table lists pre-opening costs for the businesses.

Startup Expenses Worksheet

Startup Expenses	Low	High	My Own
Rent/security deposit	$0	$2,300	625.00
Equipment	$5,000	$17,000	
Inventory	$0	$500	
Licenses and taxes	$250	$350	
Communications	$100	$250	
Payroll	$0	$4,000	-0-
Advertising/promotion	$500	$2,000	
Legal fees and accounting	$650	$1,500	
Insurance (first quarter)	$800	$1,700	550/yr
Miscellaneous	$750	$1,500	
Total	$8,050	$31,100	

Stat Fact

A thorough business plan tends to be about 25 pages long and involve 300 hours of preparation. Plan on writing this plan yourself rather than hiring a writer because you want the plan to reflect your voice and personal vision of your company. If you are not confident in your role as writer, have a freelance editor look over your finished plan for polishing any stylistic or grammatical issues.

Creating a Map for Success

To make sure you keep your business goals and strategies clearly in sight, you need a well organized and thoughtfully drafted business plan as well as a succinct and convincing mission statement.

Your Business Plan

Broadly speaking, your business plan should discuss the event planning industry,

The event planner is responsible for myriad details, right down to stemware and table center-pieces. *Photo courtesy of SignatureEventsNH.*

your business structure, the service you will offer, your clients, the competition and how you will beat it, your income and cash flow, and other relevant financial information.

A well-conceived business plan will provide you with a map for the future of your venture, as well as something by which to gauge your progress. Your plan thus becomes an operating tool that will help you manage your business. In addition, a business plan is the chief instrument you will use to communicate your ideas to others—including business people, bankers, and partners. If you seek financing for your business, the plan will become the basis for your loan proposal. Even if you don't plan to seek financing, you must take the time to write a business plan. This plan will help you to cement the logistics and growth curve of your new business.

The Components of a Successful Business Plan

Every thorough and useful business plan should contain the following seven components:

1. *Executive summary*. As the name suggests, this section summarizes your entire business plan. It includes details about the nature of your business, the type

and scope of event planning services that you will provide, the legal form of your business (covered in Chapter 4), and your vision and goals for the business.

2. *Business description.* In this section you'll describe the event planning business as a whole and your target market. Use specifics here, hard numbers, and facts. Along with those found in this guide, you'll find more event planning statistics at www.census.gov.

3. *Market strategies.* Here you will describe exactly how you will reach out to and market to prospective clients. Again, be as specific as possible. Will you advertise in the Yellow Pages? Join professional organizations for networking? Create a website? Use newsletters as a marketing device? Social media? Include as many of these details as possible. Also, take time in this section to write about the ways in which your company is unique and, therefore, better than your competitors.

4. *Competitive analysis.* In this section, focus on likely competitors in your field. Discuss how your services will differ from other event planners. Also, don't forget to focus on other potential competitors, such as hotels and banquet halls with in-house staffs to plan events. Why are your services preferable to those of your competitors? It is essential that you clearly formulate the ways in which your company will differentiate itself from competitors.

5. *Design and development plan.* This is an opportunity to discuss how you will develop markets for your business and develop an ever-broader client base. Set specific goals. Perhaps you plan to develop and hold ten social events during your first year of business and to grow that number to 25 events per year by your fifth year in the event planning business.

6. *Operations and management plan.* How will you run your business on a day-to-day basis? Will this be a part- or full-time career for you? Will you hire employees? Consider a typical day in your business and describe it here and how you will facilitate this operation.

Beware!
You may be tempted to forgo creating and writing a business plan. Don't give in to this temptation. Ask any successful business owner and she will tell you that the business plan was key to her success. A business plan helps you to envision and plan your business and is absolutely vital if you plan to seek financing.

Profile
Erin Kelley of Stargazers in Wisconsin kept her startup expenses low and plans to grow the business slowly while she raises her young family. You can start your business with basic office equipment like a computer, perhaps a fax machine, a good cell phone, and high-quality business cards.

7. *Financial factors.* This is the section in which to focus on your financial expectations. Even if you are opening the business as a very part-time occupation—for instance, planning only five events per year—you will need to forecast your financial future. Consider where you would like to be financially in one year and in five years and include that information here.

Crafting a Mission Statement

Your mission statement also plays a crucial role in giving your business every chance for success. Quite simply, a mission statement identifies, in as little as one sentence, your company's goals.

Consider the power of athletic giant Nike's mission statement: "To bring inspiration and innovation to every athlete* in the world. *If you have a body, you are an athlete." These two carefully crafted sentences give a world of information about Nike and its vision.

One way in which to consider your mission statement is to view it as a cross between a slogan and a corporate summary. As with your business plan, take time to carefully consider this statement. Make sure that you are able to remember your mission statement—if you can't remember it, then no one else will be able to either!

On a Mission

When writing a mission statement, consider these tips:

○ *Keep it brief.* One or two sentences is ideal. Never write a mission statement longer than four sentences.

○ *Answer the who, what, and why of your company.* Tell who your company is, what you do and what you stand for, and why you do it and why you have a passion for it.

○ *Look at other mission statements.* Choose a company you admire and visit its website to read the mission statement.

○ *Don't write a hyperbolic mission statement.* Write a mission statement in which you can truly believe.

A Day in the Life

This chapter covers the nuts and bolts of planning an event, outlining the steps involved and giving helpful hints.

Dr. Joe Goldblatt, CSEP, has identified what he calls the five phases of event management: research, design, planning, coordination, and evaluation. His focus is on the production of large-scale events, and he has written several books on the topic (see the

Appendix). Here we borrow his framework and adapt it to include the production of smaller events, with one vocabulary change. Because we use the term planning in this book to talk about the overall activity that includes these five phases, we will avoid confusion by referring to this phase as organization.

Stat Fact
The Center for Convention Industry Research Index reported that the third quarter of 2010 showed promise for the easing of the recession for the convention industry, with a 5.5 percent increase over the same period in 2009. The Index uses professional attendance, revenues, net square feet of exhibit space sold, and number of exhibiting companies in their measurements.

Research

The best way to reduce risk (whatever the kind) is to do your homework. For large events, research may mean making sure that there is a demand for the event. To find out this kind of information, you can conduct surveys or interviews, or you can assemble small groups of potential attendees, called focus groups, for discussion. Although you are researching demand for an event instead of demand for your business, the strategies are the same as those discussed in the market research sections in Chapter 1.

The Essentials

Successful event planners must have:

○ *Excellent oversight of a project as a whole.* Event planning is challenging in that successful event planners must have both big-picture and small-picture abilities. In other words, while planning an event for thousands and conceiving an overarching design, she must also manage literally hundreds of details.

○ *Astute time-line management abilities.* Event planners must coordinate dozens and dozens of details that must all come together at the right time. One missed cue—for instance, the DJ who shows up late—can crash the party.

○ *Vendor negotiation skills* to negotiate money-saving deals for clients.

Research can take different forms. For instance, if you are planning an event that will be held in another city, the local convention and visitors bureau should be able to help you. It can guide you to a hotel that meets your client's needs and stays within your budget. These bureaus should also have a great deal of information on local attractions and sites for meetings and conventions. Convention personnel in hotels can offer valuable suggestions, but remember that they may have their own agendas. If you intend to look for suppliers or vendors in a city you have never visited, ask for referrals from other planners who have worked there.

They may be able to direct you to excellent providers.

If you are new to the event planning industry, research may mean finding out all you can about vendors and suppliers. Of course, searching the internet is a great way to start. As you meet with potential vendors, note which events they specialize in and how much they charge. Even if you decide during the interview that you won't use their services right away, you should still take notes for future reference. Industry expert, author, and consultant Patty Sachs recommends using small cards and filing them in a box divided into main-event supplier categories. If you prefer your computer for this kind of thing, start a favorites folder for each type of vendor—you still will want to take notes, so start a corresponding word processing program file for each of the vendors in your favorites list. Sachs cautions owners to note prices, style numbers, lead time, contact persons, and anything else that seems pertinent, even if you don't use the vendor for that particular event. "You are as good as your Rolodex," she advises. For more information on hiring vendors, see Chapter 6.

Research also may mean talking to other planners who have produced events similar to the one on which you are working. Or you may find yourself reading up on issues of custom and etiquette, especially if you are unfamiliar with a particular type of event.

Whatever kind of event you are planning, research should include asking

Smart Tip

Tip...

All the event planners interviewed for this book agree that word of mouth is the ideal way in which to find the best vendors. Ask other event planners, as well as those who have recently held events, to recommend vendors. It's likely you'll find the same vendor names coming up time and time again.

your client a lot of questions and writing down the answers. New York City planner Jaclyn Bernstein, Destination Management Certified Professional (DMCP), works primarily with clients from out of town. To avoid communication problems, she makes sure she knows what the client's goals are and how the client thinks the event should be handled. "Try to use the client's exact words in your proposal," she suggests.

Always find out what customers hope to accomplish with an event. Do they want to introduce a new product, motivate employees, or provide a forum for networking? Do they want to put together a spectacular college reunion? Do they want to celebrate their parents' anniversary with an unforgettable party? Clients may want an event that is strictly business, strictly social, or somewhere in between.

Interviewing a client may not be what you immediately think of as research. However, asking too few questions or not listening adequately to a client's answers can compromise the success of the event you plan. Also, be sure to ask the right type of questions, questions that allow the respondents to clearly express their preferences. Questions with simple "yes" or "no" answers will tend to be less helpful to your planning process.

When planning, you'll need to garner the following information:

1. *Who?* Who are the attendees, and how many of them will be at the event (a dozen company executives, 30 children, 80 elderly ping-pong enthusiasts)?

2. *What?* What kind of event will this be (a family reunion, an elegant sit-down banquet, a fashionable but laid-back art show reception)? Don't forget to ask about the style of the event (formal, relaxed, traditional, avant garde, etc.), and whether your client wants a theme event (see discussion below).

3. *When?* Find out the date of the event.

4. *Where?* The client may want you to suggest a venue for the event, but you should always find out what type of location is desired (something unusual, informal, elegant, indoors or outdoors?).

5. *Why?* Find out the reason for the event. What is the client's goal or objective?

6. *How?* How does the client want guests to remember the event? As the most original picnic they've ever been to? As a holiday evening filled with one surprise after another? As a company party with the best food they've had in a long time? The issue of how guests should remember an occasion is crucial in deciding which aspects of the event should be given priority. Recognizing that

By Invitation Only

Any invitations you send potential attendees should include the following information:

- ◯ Event
- ◯ Host's name
- ◯ Date
- ◯ Time
- ◯ Location
- ◯ RSVP phone number or e-mail
- ◯ RSVP deadline

Optional elements include the following:

- ◯ Significance of the event (purpose, frequency, historic importance)
- ◯ Dress requirements
- ◯ Directions and parking instructions
- ◯ Names of prominent speakers
- ◯ VIP status
- ◯ Complimentary ticket enclosure

Always give attendees a deadline for responding to announcements if they must confirm attendance. This will ensure that you meet your own deadlines. If you fail to conclude arrangements for airfare or hotel rooms in time, you will lose discounts offered for advance reservations.

few clients have unlimited funds, always find out what aspects of the event your customer feels are most important.

And, unlike a reporter, you must always add the crucial additional question:

7. *How much?* In other words, what is the available budget? This piece of information will affect your event design, because many ideas will not be possible to achieve with the funds available. Telling clients that what they want is impossible

Staying on Top of Trends

Key to your success will be staying on top of event planning trends. Current trends include:

○ *Green events.* The trend is toward planning parties with an eye on protecting the environment, from biodegradable, potato-based flatware to organic menus and limousines fueled by electricity.

○ *Catering stations.* Many clients prefer catering stations rather than serving sit-down dinners. Businesses find that as attendees fill their plates at stations, they tend to network and make better connections than at more formal events.

○ *Streamlined events.* The emphasis is on doing more with less and on working smarter. Event attendees lead busy lives, and, particularly when planning corporate events, you will need to keep attendees moving and keep the day concentrated.

○ *Heritage-related events.* Festivals of all kinds remain popular.

○ *Local events.* Companies are doing what they can to reduce the need for travel. Instead of one large national event, some corporations now hold several regional events.

○ *"Recycled" events.* There has been a recent increase in party-pooling (i.e., two or more hosts combining their resources to produce an event) and repeat parties (i.e., reusing decor for another party the following day).

Planning Trends

○ *Concern for charities.* Recently, organizers of social events (e.g., birthday parties) have requested guest donations to charity in lieu of gifts. Both corporations and individuals often donate leftover food to local homeless shelters and food banks.

○ *Accessibility for the disabled.* The Americans with Disabilities Act requires that all publicly accessible buildings accommodate disabled people, including wheelchair space, ramps, handrails, a clear line of sight between audience and sign-language interpreter, and appropriate table heights. Many planners go even beyond what is now required by law.

○ *Responsible drinking.* This trend has resulted in decreased amounts of alcohol at events and in the provision of designated drivers.

given their budget is not a job for the fainthearted. On the other hand, remember that anyone who chooses to plan events is both stouthearted and has nerves made of steel! Just make sure you are tactful so that the client won't run off, never to knock at your door again.

> ## Bright Idea
>
> As a first step in social event planning, consultant Patty Sachs suggests providing every potential client with a sheet that briefly details how your company works, what the general price structure is like, etc. This strategy ensures that clients are aware you'll require a deposit and that your company does not produce events for $10 per hour!

Once you have noted answers to the basic seven questions, you need more specific information. Do your clients want to have any live entertainment at the event? What kind? What type of food and beverages would they like? How elaborate must the props or decorations be? Do they want a photographer or videographer? Will transportation be needed? Should there be valet parking?

Add these details to your notebook. Or make copies of the Event Design Worksheet, starting on page 41, and fill one out for each event.

Adequate research is important to the success of any event you plan. Yet Goldblatt finds that the research phase often does not receive enough attention. Make sure you have asked and received answers to all the above questions before you proceed to the design phase.

Design Time

Your creativity comes most into play in the design phase of event planning, during which you sketch out the overall feel and look of the event. This is the time to brainstorm, either by yourself or with your employees. It's also the time to pull out and look through your idea file. (You do have one, don't you? If not, read on and take notes.) Don't forget to consult your notebook for the client's answers to the questions you asked in the research phase. These responses, especially the one regarding the event budget, will help you to thoroughly check each idea for feasibility, preferably before suggesting it to the client.

Developing Design Ideas

Sachs has the following suggestions for ensuring you are never stumped for design ideas to build on. "Attend openings, promotions, shows, and other events to study the way that they are produced," she says. "Save invitations and programs. Make 'event idea' cards, and file them in a box according to category."

If you are stumped for ideas to propose to your client, consider a theme event, which is always popular. Themes may be inspired by a variety of factors, including time (Roaring Twenties, Medieval Festival, Disco Days), place (Caribbean Island, Outer Space), hobbies (Night at the Theater, Spa Party, Tennis Mixer), or special events (Indy 500, Academy Awards, Super Bowl).

Elements of Style

The design phase is the time to pay close attention to the style of the event. If the client wants an elegant banquet with Victorian accents, sites like a giant hayloft or a space museum aren't good bets. (Yes, we know that's an extreme example, but you get the point.) On the other hand, a boating party followed by an open-air picnic, while not the first type of event that springs to mind, might work extremely well if the site, décor, catering, and entertainment fit the style of the event. The rest of our discussion of the design phase will focus on the four aspects of the event style, including site selection, décor, catering, and entertainment.

Tents offer great options and creativity in designing outdoor events. *Photo courtesy of SignatureEventsNH.*

Selecting a Site

Your choice of site will depend on several factors. Chief among these are your client, the event budget, and the purpose of the event. Corporate events, meetings, and conventions typically take place in hotels, convention centers, meeting centers, clients' facilities, or restaurants. More elaborate corporate events may take place at exotic sites, such as on cruise ships or in resorts.

Social events can be held virtually anywhere your imagination (or your client's) will go. Possible event sites include the following:

- Fresh air (garden or park, farm or ranch, forest or meadow, backyard, beach, or lake-front)
- On the move (ship or yacht, train, double-decker bus, trolley)
- Home, sweet home (house, mansion, castle)
- Child's play (zoo, theme park, children's restaurant, circus, children's theater, art center)
- Cultured pearls (university, museum, planetarium, symphony hall)
- Good sports (swimming pool, miniature golf course, baseball diamond, skating rink, tennis club)

When looking at sites, remember that price is one of many factors to consider. Look at the entire package of amenities and services offered. Make sure you understand what is included in price quotes. Some sites include taxes and service charges in their quotes while others do not. Keep in mind that a site with a low-end quote may turn out to be more expensive than one with a high-end quote if the former charges for services the latter offers for free. Carefully compare services and prices. Consultant Patty Sachs offers an additional piece of advice: "Get the reactions of others who have rented the site for events."

Creating the Perfect Décor

Creativity is a key element in this aspect of event planning. For this reason, the décor profit margin can be as much as 40 percent for a large, elaborate event. If you are handling the décor yourself, remember to allow for the creative work involved. Do not give clients estimates until you are sure of what they want and how much time and effort you will spend to achieve it.

Perhaps your strength as a planner is in your ability to handle the myriad details involved in organizing the event, but you feel less confident in your ability to design

Beware!
Many sites have restrictions. Historic sites, for instance, may have limits on the types of décor. Other sites may not allow alcohol to be served. Don't set yourself and your client up for a nasty surprise. Always thoroughly check that a location offers all the amenities your client requires. Remember, too, that if the site is outdoors, you'll need to make provisions for electricity, water, and restroom facilities, as well as for shelter from inclement weather.

décor. Then don't be afraid to ask others for help. Work with florists and caterers who can not only help you design for specific events but also help you to build your own design sense.

Décor elements can include, but are not limited to, the following:

- Constructed set elements (castle, bridge, storefront)
- Painted backdrops (mural, play scenery)
- Props (fountain, trellis, palm trees, furniture)
- Fabric displays (swags, drapes)
- Floral treatments (centerpieces, greenery drapes, garlands, bouquets)
- Lighting elements (spotlight, strobes, small white lights)
- Historical elements (period pieces, documents)
- Signage (banner, signposts)
- Guests themselves (period costumes, for example)
- Accessories (candles, balloons)

Simply Beautiful

Liese Gardner and Susan Terpening, authors of *The Art of Event Design* (Premedia Business Magazines & Media Inc.), provide the following décor tips:

○ To make a bold statement, consider a black-and-white color scheme, adding a fashionable accent color for flair.

○ Scale is very important. If possible, use huge décor elements at entranceways to create an impact and a sense of enormous space.

○ Skillful repetition is also key to successful design. But use your instincts, and avoid repeating your main elements too many times.

○ Streamline your event décor by looking at all elements of the design and taking away anything that's not absolutely necessary. Remember, less is more!

Depending on the size of the event, your own background, and how important each element of the décor is judged to be, you may have separate vendors for each element or you may do it all yourself.

If you are doing the décor yourself, remember to pay extra attention to the entrance and reception areas. These are the areas that make the first impression and where the majority of photographs will be taken. Lighting is often a neglected décor element; not only is it extremely important to mood and ambiance but it can, in fact, be the single most important element of an event. Lighting is also useful for creating special effects and for enhancing themes.

The goal of the event and the age of its attendees both help determine the use of space in terms of décor and seating arrangements. For example, if the main purpose is to provide networking opportunities, then guests need to be able to move around freely, and the event site should be relatively free of chairs and other potential obstacles. On the other hand, if the attendees are all senior citizens, extra seating will be needed to ensure comfort.

Food, Glorious Food

Food and beverages have a well-established role in successful events. Experts have identified a trend involving increased attention to the nutritional value of foods. In addition, food presentation (i.e., the way food looks in a display or on a plate) is receiving a lot of attention. The French have said it for centuries: "C'est la presentation qui compte" ("Presentation is what counts"). The rest of us are only now catching on. If you are planning small events, you are less likely to encounter food sculptures or other more elaborate presentation effects, but always make sure you hire a caterer who not only pays attention to the taste and nutritional content of food, but also provides a variety of food colors and textures.

If you discuss food choices with clients, you will undoubtedly consider customer preference and budget. Also keep in mind the following aspects of the event:

Smart Tip

Tip...

When it comes to food, trends seem to develop more quickly than the proverbial eye blink, so it is essential that you keep your ear to the ground—or in this case, to the kitchen door—to stay on top of the foodie "ins" and "outs." For instance, remember when green tea was the hip, healthy drink? Those days are over. Hipsters are drinking yerba matte from Argentina, the "new green tea." Keep in tune by reading the food section of your local paper, by subscribing to the food magazines of your choice, and by checking out what the hot new restaurants in your area are serving. Staying on top of culinary news will give you a competitive edge.

Thinking Outside the Box ... or Basket!

When a seasonal club approached Lauren Polastri to plan their summer events, she had to think outside the box:

"I was approached by this huge yacht club with very limited kitchen and cooking facilities. They didn't want a buffet. In the past, they felt that the lines had been too long and that buffets weren't appropriate for some of their black-tie events. They also had a very set budget. So, I came up with an idea to use baskets. Each table of 10 or 12 guests is presented with a beautiful basket, overflowing with food. For instance, at the 4th of July party, the basket was filled with lovely foods like filet mignon; shrimp kabobs; and potato, green bean, and pasta salads. The baskets are passed around each table. It's very social and interactive since people have to speak to one another as the basket is passed, and it's an elegant way to present the food. It also means no more standing in long buffet lines! Now, I am having brides ask for the same presentation—using baskets at each table."

- *Formality.* Simpler foods work best with relaxed occasions. Reserve fancier food items for more formal events.
- *Theme or region.* If the event has a theme, match the food to it. When appropriate, consider regional cuisine.
- *Seating plan.* Foods requiring a knife and fork are best reserved for sit-down events. If guests will be standing, such as at a cocktail party, finger foods are preferable. Finger foods should be bite-sized.
- *Overall "look" of serving stations or tables.* As noted above, food color is important to the presentation effect. A banquet choice of chicken, mashed potatoes, cauliflower, and white rolls suffers from several problems, among which is that all these items are white! Encourage clients to choose foods with vivid colors like red, orange, and purple. (Yes, purple. And no, we are not suggesting dyed foods—purple cabbage makes a terrific garnish.)

Tip...

Smart Tip
Fountains remain popular design elements, including chocolate fondue fountains and trendy fountains serving Cosmopolitans.

That's Entertainment

The possibilities for entertaining guests are virtually limitless. Keep in mind that usually the more involved the guests are, the better time they'll have. Just to get you started, here are a few ideas:

- Performing arts (dancers, musicians, singers, actors, comedians)
- Mysticism (fortune tellers, palm readers, magicians)
- Circus (clowns, acrobats, jugglers, tightrope walkers)
- Interactive (caricaturist)
- Carnival (games, rides)
- Kids' fun (puppets, mimes, robots, ventriloquists, balloon artists, petting zoo)
- Pastimes and sports (croquet, horseshoes, miniature golf, volleyball)
- Period performances (jousting, chariot races, wandering minstrels)

The Main Event

Once you have interviewed the client and done some preliminary brainstorming, you should have enough information to fill out the Event Design Worksheet starting on page 41.

If you are just starting out in the event planning industry, make sure you have this worksheet or something similar filled out before you provide the client with a proposal containing an event cost estimate (see Chapter 10). Note that your proposal need not detail every aspect of the event design.

Be aware that the production of a proposal is time consuming and potentially expensive, especially if you include photographs or sketches. Sachs points out that only the larger companies producing high-end events can afford to provide clients free proposals. You should receive a consultation fee (she suggests about $150), which can be applied toward a client's event if he or she hires you.

Maximizing the appeal of an event means making sure that all five senses are

Tip...

Smart Tip

Include emergency phone numbers in your event records in case problems arise. Suppliers and any vendors not on-site for the event should give you numbers to call if, for example, any equipment malfunctions. Also, store these phone numbers in your cell phone for one-touch dialing.

▲

Seating Chart

The following are the typical seating configurations for different event types:

○ *Banquet rounds.* This is the most frequently used seating for social functions involving food. Round tables are 60 or 72 inches in diameter and normally seat from 8 to 12 people.

○ *Reception.* Smaller round tables with cocktail and food stations throughout a room.

○ *One long oval or rectangular table.* This type of table is ideal for small parties or meetings in which close interaction is desired.

○ *U-shape, T-shape, and E-shape; hollow square; and hollow circle styles.* These configurations are all created using 8-foot-long tables. These seating plans are ideal for committee or staff meetings.

○ *Classroom-, theater-, or auditorium-style.* Rows of chairs face the front of the room, either with or without desks. This seating style is used for corporate events involving presentations.

engaged—but not overwhelmed. Goldblatt suggests providing not only sensory areas but also "neutral zones" whenever possible, especially if the event is a large one. Before finalizing the design, you should mentally "walk through" the event. What will guests see, hear, smell, taste, and touch?

Once you have a signed contract and a design that meets client approval, it is time to organize the details of the event.

All-Important Organization

During this decision-intensive phase, you will rent the site, hire vendors, and take care of even more details than you might believe possible. You'll be on the phone until your ear is numb. But before you do any of this, make sure you have a contact person (either the client or someone acting on the client's behalf) with whom you'll discuss all major decisions. Ideally, this person's name should appear on the client agreement (see Chapter 4). Having a designated individual helps ensure that communication lines are kept open. Also, social events in particular sometimes suffer from the "too many

Measuring Up

Use the following industry tips to help gauge serving requirements:

❍ A gallon of liquid (punch, coffee, etc.) fills approximately 20 standard (8-oz.) cups.

❍ As a general rule, 30 percent of the coffee you provide should be decaffeinated and 70 percent regular, except in the evening, when the numbers are closer to 50 percent each.

❍ Assuming a comfortable room temperature at the event venue, 65 percent of morning beverages should be hot and 35 percent cold. In the afternoon, beverages should be 35 percent hot and 65 percent cold. Guidelines are more difficult in the evening when the beverages offered depend greatly on the type of event.

❍ Provide one server for every 20 to 25 people at a sit-down meal.

❍ Provide one bartender for every 75 to 100 people, unless the event is primarily for cocktails. In that case, you may need one bartender for every 25 to 30 guests.

cooks" syndrome. Having one designated contact helps you avoid being caught in the middle of disagreements. "You don't want to find yourself caught between mother and daughter or husband and wife," says Sachs.

Generally speaking, the bigger the event, the more lead time is required to plan it. Major conventions are planned years in advance. Although you may not be arranging events on such a grand scale, you do need to allow at least a few months for events like corporate picnics, reunions, or large parties.

Begin by arranging for the following:

• *Site*. If applicable, you must have a signed contract for the site before any other plans can be made. Do not

Smart Tip

Tip...

Be sure to have a headset for both your home phone and your cell phone. Many states now require headsets for drivers using their cell phones. As an event planner, you will spend many hours on the phone, making a headset a must-have piece of equipment.

proceed with your planning until you have locked up the site location.

- *Air travel.* If your client's event requires it, air travel arrangements should be made as soon as possible after signing the site contract. With sufficient lead time, you can usually obtain group rates from most major airlines. Select a company that has experience with group travel and can advise you of the lowest fares available and the best routes for your attendees. Again, the sooner you purchase tickets, generally the greater the savings you'll realize for your client.

Beware!
Unfortunately, there are some limousine companies that have proved to be less than reliable. For instance, they might send cars with malfunctioning air conditioners on the muggiest day of the summer. Help to ensure first-rate limousine service by checking with the National Limousine Association at www.limo.org.

- *Ground transportation.* Depending on the event and the number of attendees, you may need to contract with a limousine service, a bus company, a car rental agency, or even a trolley company to meet your needs. Normally, planners should arrange for attendee transportation to and from the airport, for guided tours, and to special events outside the site. Before you choose ground transportation services, compare the reservation, deposit, payment, and cancellation policies of several companies to make sure you get the best service.

- *Vendors.* Make sure you have done your homework and that you possess signed contracts.

Organization Checklist

Once these major decisions have been made, you will have many more details to deal with. Starting on page 44, there's a checklist to help you, although you may not need to do all these things. Time frames are shown in a range to accommodate a variety of event sizes. Use this checklist and fill in any other tasks particular to your event.

Balancing the Logistics

Effective organization requires logistical ability and knowledge of the following types of information, among others:

- How many people can you comfortably get into a room? This depends on the purpose of the event, the activities involved, and the space taken up by the décor.

Event Design Worksheet

1. *Who?*
   Type of guest: _____
   Age group: _____
   Number of guests: _____
   Degree of guest participation: _____

2. *What?*
   Type of event: _____
   _____
   Style: _____
   _____
   Theme? _____
   _____

3. *When?*
   Date: _____
   Start time: _____
   End time: _____
   Invitations to be sent? _____

4. *Where?*
   Site (or site type): _____
   Guest lodging to be arranged? _____
   Transport to be arranged? _____
   Security services needed? _____
   Emergency personnel needed? _____
   Special needs to be accommodated? _____

5. *Why?*
   Goal/purpose of the event: _____
   _____
   Publicity for the event? _____
   _____
   _____

Event Design Worksheet, continued

6. *How?*

   How should guests remember the event? (Prioritize the following.)

   ○ *Site*

   Type of facility: _____

   Location: _____

   Accommodations: _____

   Amenities: _____

   ○ *Décor*

   Major elements: _____

   _____

   Additional elements: _____

   _____

   ○ *Catering*

   Type of cuisine: _____

   Beverages/alcohol: _____

   Type of service (cocktail, buffet, seated table service): _____

   _____

   ○ *Entertainment*

   Music: _____

   _____

   Performance: _____

   _____

   Activities: _____

   _____

   Speaker: _____

   _____

7. *How Much?*

   What is the budget? _____

   Range of flexibility? _____

   _____

   _____

   _____

- Will one buffet line service 350 people? (It won't!)
- Where will food service stations be placed? Put them in areas with easy access for replenishing.
- How long to allow for a cocktail reception? Allow 30 minutes to an hour.
- How to let guests know to begin eating? An invocation or some other cue should do the trick.
- How to be sure guests will have finished eating before the scheduled activities begin? Build in a little extra time.

Coordinating the Event

After you have made the initial plans, turn your attention to each of the activities that form a part of the overall event. At this point, your goal is to ensure that everyone is on the same wavelength. Good communication skills are important. Make sure all vendors have at least a general idea of the overall event schedule. Even more important, vendors should be clear about what is expected of them, and when. Vendor arrival times should appear in the contracts, but verify those times anyway. This is a "check and recheck" period. Make sure all your staff members know their roles. Remember, good communication is key. "Big projects can get out of control very quickly," cautions planner Joyce Barnes-Wolff.

Use a notebook (or your computer) to track the progress of each aspect of the event. While you will not record items that a vendor is responsible for providing (e.g., flowers ordered by the florist or food items the caterer orders), your tracking system should include all supplies and equipment your own business orders, as well as the names of suppliers, so you can verify them quickly. Use separate lists for items purchased and rented. The Organization Checklist on page 44 is a sample of the information you might want to include in your records.

To maximize the effectiveness of your coordination efforts—not to mention minimize your headaches—remember:

- Delegate when possible.
- Anticipate change and be flexible.
- Have a backup plan for any critical aspects of the event.

Smart Tip

Tip...

As this chapter illustrates, event planning is a virtual juggling act. You are project manager, coordinator, creative designer, and more. Because of the immense detail required to plan any event, keep careful notes. You may be tempted to forgo this process, thinking you can keep certain details stored in your mind rather than on paper. Don't be tempted. What isn't written down is likely to become lost.

Organization Checklist

Stage I (30–90 days before the event)

- ❏ Reserve venue and accommodations
- ❏ Review budget (periodically)
- ❏ Contract with vendors
- ❏ Investigate licensing requirements
- ❏ Develop a marketing plan, if needed
- ❏ Make note of can't-miss dates in vendor contracts
- ❏ Invite speakers (after confirming availability)
- ❏ Schedule entertainment
- ❏ Send announcements or invitations to attendees
- ❏ Select audiovisual materials
- ❏ Contact suppliers of any items you handle yourself (e.g., rental items)

Stage II (15–60 days before the event)

- ❏ Send second announcements with information on hotel and travel arrangements
- ❏ Complete the activities list and the menus
- ❏ Verify arrangements with client, vendors, and suppliers
- ❏ Complete contingency/emergency plans
- ❏ Prepare evaluations
- ❏ Prepare list of temporary help needed

Stage III (10–30 days before the event)

- ❏ Finalize event setups, transportation, and guest accommodations
- ❏ Confirm reservation of audiovisual equipment
- ❏ Arrange for transport of audiovisual equipment to the site
- ❏ Submit a room list and pay a deposit to the site
- ❏ Complete airline reservations
- ❏ Hire temporary help

Organization Checklist, continued

❏ Conduct orientation meeting/training of temporary help

❏ Send any event-related tickets to attendees

Stage IV (5–10 days before the event)

❏ Send all printed materials to the site (keep master copies for yourself in case materials are lost)

❏ Contact all vendors to confirm

- Share critical timing elements with vendors and site personnel.

Another way to minimize your headaches is to use a checklist like the one on page 47.

"You Cannot Rest on Your Laurels"

As all event planners will tell you, "You're only as good as your last event." Lauren Polastri, of The Other Woman, agrees. "You absolutely cannot rest on your laurels. You need to be fresh and energized for every event."

One crucial test of an event's success is customer satisfaction. The goal, of course, is to end up with a client who will sing your praises up and down the street, shouting it from rooftops. This is the client who will hire you again, perhaps for an even bigger (and more expensive) event. This is also the customer who will provide the famous word-of-mouth advertising for you.

Having a blissfully happy client does not mean you're home free, however. You can always improve, and additional evaluation will help you to do so. If you have employees, a round-table post-event discussion can bring to light aspects you may not have considered. Collect input from every team member. Your evaluation procedure should include an actualization, i.e., an accounting of your company's investment (hours worked, costs incurred) in the event. This procedure helps verify that you are charging clients enough to make a profit.

There are several other ways to evaluate the success of an event. One is to have a trained individual observe it and give you feedback. Such an individual could be an event planning consultant. Depending on the consultant's experience level and the type of event, you can expect to pay anywhere from $25 to $50 per hour, for 10 or more hours. A shorter session would probably mean a higher hourly rate.

This individual could also be a lay person, however. If you know someone who hosts extremely successful parties, consider asking that person to observe your event. Or get someone who plans fundraising events to help you in return for a generous donation.

Another way to evaluate an event is to get feedback from other industry professionals working at the event. The caterer and the bartender, among others, might be able to provide you with suggestions.

If the event is open to the general public (e.g., a community event), consider surveying the guests at the event. You can get immediate feedback this way, and most people you approach will cooperate. Talk to as many people as time allows, and take notes. Remember, the feedback you receive may not be very balanced. People may be

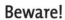

Beware!

Lauren Polastri of The Other Woman learned the hard way about confirming the delivery of rental items. "I arrived at a small event and found that the items that were to be delivered the day before had not arrived. Fortunately, I was able to send one of my employees to pick everything up and the day was saved. I learned to always check on rentals the day before. Make sure the numbers are correct and that everything is clean and in good condition. Rentals can absolutely make or break an event."

swept up in the mood of the moment. Without time for them to step back and reflect, they may provide unwarrantedly positive or negative feedback. Conducting a mail or phone survey can eliminate this disadvantage, but you will not get the same level of cooperation. A response rate of 10 percent is considered average, so you will need to survey many more guests than you would with a face-to-face survey.

However you conduct your survey, keep your questions to a minimum and keep them short. You can have people fill out the sample survey on page 48 at the event, or you could mail it to attendees.

Sample Tracking Record—Items Rented

Item	Quantity	Use	Supplier	Date Received	Cost (Total)
linens-round	30	tables	AJ Linens	7/15/XX	$174.80
linens-rect.	10	buffet tables	AJ Linens	7/15/XX	$35.67
lanterns	25	lighting (grounds)	Lux Inc.	not received	$150.00

Coordination Checklist

Stage I (Day before the event)

- ❏ Review the program with site directors
- ❏ Troubleshoot with staff to overcome any problems
- ❏ Confirm arrival of all printed and audiovisual materials
- ❏ Confirm delivery of all rental items (or else pick them up)
- ❏ Tour the facility to confirm setups
- ❏ Ensure that all vendors' contact numbers are stored in your cell phone

Stage II (Day of the event)

- ❏ Check signage
- ❏ Verify that all rental items have arrived—tick them off
- ❏ Inspect all setups at least one hour before the event begins, checking off items in your notebook
- ❏ Test all microphones and audiovisual equipment
- ❏ Distribute evaluations at the event

Stage III (After the event)

- ❏ Return any kegs and recover deposits
- ❏ Distribute tips
- ❏ Write thank-you letters to client, site personnel, and vendors
- ❏ Review and approve all vendor bills for payment
- ❏ Have post-event evaluation meeting (it is important to have this meeting while the event is still fresh in everyone's mind)
- ❏ Compile all event data in one file and store in records

Whatever combination of strategies you choose, Goldblatt advises, don't wait until the end of the event before collecting at least some feedback. Unless you know about them in time, it's impossible to correct details that might make the difference between an average event and a stand-out one.

Sample Survey

Please rate the following aspects of this event by circling your response:

1. *Décor*	Excellent	Good	Average	Fair	Poor
2. *Food/beverage*	Excellent	Good	Average	Fair	Poor
3. *Entertainment*	Excellent	Good	Average	Fair	Poor
4. *Service*	Excellent	Good	Average	Fair	Poor
5. *Friendliness of personnel*	Excellent	Good	Average	Fair	Poor
6. *Service*	Excellent	Good	Average	Fair	Poor

We appreciate any comments you can provide:

_____

_____

_____

Thank you for your help!

Finally, carefully consider the evaluation. Don't simply tuck the responses in your desk drawer. Some of the evaluations may sting a bit if they are critical, but view these criticisms as constructive and make plans to address these issues at your next event. This attention to detail could enable you to take your events from so-so to smashing successes.

Now that you know what is involved in each stage of the event planning process, we turn our attention to what you need to do to get your business up and running. So grab a strong cup of coffee, or a large chocolate bar, or both. Then read on as we tackle the necessary paperwork.

Getting Started

This chapter details much of what you will need to do before you open your doors. We will cover naming your business, determining its business structure, and finding a location. We will also take a brief pass at acquiring the necessary licenses, permits, and business insurance. (Well, you didn't expect every aspect

▲

to be fascinating, did you?) Finally, we will provide some sample documents you'll need to run your business.

It's All in a Name

There is no question that the right name can draw your target market to you. It can also single out your event planning business from others and keep it sharp in clients' memories. Before you decide on a name, consider what kind of planning you want to do, the scope you want your business to have, and whether you want to convey a particular image. Will you have a highly specialized service (e.g., only birthday parties) or an extremely general one (e.g., social and corporate events of all kinds)? Will your service be local, national, or international? Do you want to produce only high-budget events, or will you work in any price range? Depending on your answers to these questions, a good name for your business could consist of any of the following:

- Description of your service (e.g., Event Planning Inc.)
  Advantages: Helps potential clients hone in on you.
  Disadvantages: Creativity sometimes suffers.

- The type of event you specialize in (e.g., Birthday Bashes)
  Advantages: Helps clients find you. You'll get fewer calls for types of events that you don't plan.
  Disadvantages: Your specialization might change. What if you decide to do anniversary parties, too?

- Your name (e.g., Ann Smith Inc.)
  Advantages: People you meet while networking need remember only your name. If you use your full name, you may improve your personal credit rating as you build your business.
  Disadvantages: Customers won't know what type of business this is. Worse, the IRS could confuse you and your company. And if your company goes under, your personal credit rating may suffer. Finally, if you choose to sell your business at some point, your name will become a liability. Prospective buyers prefer to buy a company that is not associated with a specific name. If Jane Doe were to buy this company and then change the name to Jane Doe Inc., she would lose the name recognition that Ann Smith worked to build. Although you may not envision selling your company, you may at some point consider a career

Smart Tip

Tip...

From smartphone apps to iPads to Twitter marketing to cell phone credit card processing, be prepared to use technology in your event planning business. Your clients and event attendees are using it and they expect you to be too!

change and choose to sell your event planning business.

- Qualities your business embodies (e.g., Elegant Evenings)

  Advantages: Helps establish the image you want to create.

  Disadvantages: Vagueness may make it tough for clients to find you. Also, this kind of name pigeonholes your

► Planning Business

Smart T

Make sure
select is no
tive. For ins
"Unforgetta
are limiting
those throw
Choose a na
a broader sc

The Name Game

After you've short-listed some ideas, ask yourself the following questions about each name:

- ❍ *Is it easy to pronounce?* People are reluctant to say a name when they're unsure of its pronunciation. This reluctance could be fatal in an industry that relies heavily on word-of-mouth advertising.

- ❍ *Is it short enough?* Length affects ease of pronunciation. Plus, you and your employees will have to say this name all day on the phone and still have time to do other tasks. Thus Supercallifragilistickexpial delicious Inc. is probably not the best choice, even if you specialize in children's events. (This name suffers from other problems, too, but we won't go into those.)

- ❍ *Is it easy and logical to spell?* If somebody hears your company name but can't find it in the phone book because of a spelling problem, you will lose potential clients. For this reason—and others—don't opt for a silly spelling of a common word. For instance, don't even think of a name like Kountry Kids Parties. Clients looking under "c" for country will be frustrated and unlikely to find your listing.

- ❍ *Is it memorable?* If possible, avoid a name that sounds too ordinary. Steer clear of hyperbole, though. Names should be meaningful and substantive.

When you have selected a name, take the time to make sure the name is not trademarked by another company. Even if you plan to keep your event planning business small, it is a good idea to check for trademarks. You can do this for free at ww.uspto.gov. Also, check popular search engines like Google and Yahoo! to see if the name you have chosen is already used for another website.

You'll probably ~~be~~ hired to produce a ~~re~~union or picnic.

- Indications of the scope of your business (e.g., Bloomington Event Planners Ltd.)

  Advantages: Anyone looking under city listings will find you.

  Disadvantages: Your scope might change. What if you want to branch out to other cities?

- A combination of the above (e.g., Benden's Classic Parties)

  Advantages and disadvantages: The whole is not necessarily the sum of the parts. Consider carefully the advantages and disadvantages of each part of a combination name to see which apply.

The outline above is not an exhaustive one, but it contains some of the best ideas for creating a name that will make your

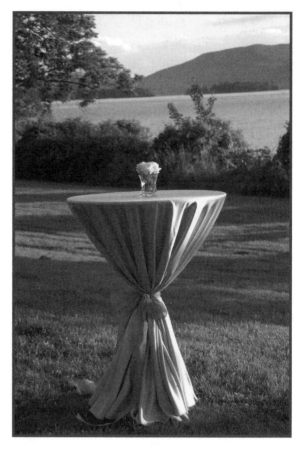

Event planner Amy Piper of SignatureEvents in New Hampshire, finds that many clients love the elegant look of highboy tables draped with steamed linens tied with a sash. *Photo courtesy of SignatureEventsNH.*

business a standout in event planning. Industry expert and consultant Patty Sachs cautions against limiting yourself by choosing too specific a name. Words like perfect, elegant, and exquisite lock you into formal or high-priced events, she says. Exciting words like fabulous, fantastic, and incredible are reserved for theme parties and entertaining events. On the other hand, if you're going to be highly specialized, she suggests names like Open House Planning, His 'n Hers Parties, Wedding Weekends, and so on. Also, she cautions, "The word 'affair' has been done to death."

Lauren Polastri, of The Other Woman event planning (www.theotherwomancaterer. com), took her name from a customer. Before she officially launched her business, she did some event planning for a friend and neighbor. He started referring to her as "the other woman," and the name stuck. Polastri says her dad warned her that the

Registering Your Company Name

Most states mandate that you register your fictitious company name officially to ensure that it is unique. This is generally done through the county and is known as filing a DBA ("doing business as") statement. If the name you chose is already being used, you will be asked to choose something else. For this reason, it's a good idea to have a backup name or two. There is a nominal ($30–$60) cost for this service.

name might be off-putting to some clients, but she has found that customers like the good humor of this name and that the name reflects the good nature and energy she brings to her successful business.

Many event planners select a name that will put them at the top of an alphabetical listing, for instance in the telephone directory. Check your local listings to see if this works for your business. AAA Event Planning may position your listing in first place, but the name is not very informative. Don't sacrifice content for this prime position.

Bright Idea

Stop periodically and write out two lists: a "Priorities in my business life" list and an "Actual time spent" list. Compare the lists. Are you spending the greater proportion of your working life on the activities to which you give a high ranking? If not, maybe it's time to reorganize.

If you buy an existing business, you can take an element from the business's former name, or even use the whole name. New York City planner Jaclyn Bernstein, DMCP, kept half of the former name when she took over an event planning business. Thus her company's name had both a familiar ring for clients and enough of a difference to remind them that ownership had changed.

A good name is well worth the effort you'll put into finding it. With some thought, you can end up with a name as unique as your business.

Choosing a Business Location

The type of events you'll plan and the size of your business are among the factors that will determine where you set up shop. Event planning businesses can be run from home, in retail or commercial space, or from a vehicle.

▲

Office Location Pointers

Whatever your location, consider the following points:

○ Planners of local parties do well in central locations.

○ Convention planners should locate near the major convention sites and hotels in their cities; similarly, a meeting planner should be situated in a central business district.

○ If you plan nonlocal events, your proximity to an airport may be paramount.

If you're starting small, a homebased event planning business may be the ideal choice for you. This option keeps overhead low and saves travel time to and from the office. One potential problem is that friends and family might drop in at all hours because you're "not really working." Be firm. Set up business hours and stick to them.

You may find that you need more space than your home office can provide. In this case, retail or commercial space can be the perfect setup for you, especially if you expect to have some foot traffic or if you specialize in a particular type of event. Deborah Williams and Kim Quigley, who plan both corporate and social events, decided to locate their business in the now-trendy Deep Ellum, a historical, artsy area of Dallas. Jaclyn Bernstein maintains her business in a fast-paced business district in midtown Manhattan. This location is important for her company because she focuses on corporate events.

The disadvantage of renting space is primarily the cost. Rent, utilities, and parking are all considerable expenses. Downtown locations are especially costly.

Commercial leases are often more complicated than residential leases. Before signing, check with an attorney. Commercial leases are difficult to break, so proceed with caution.

Executive suites also make sense for event planning businesses. They provide you with a good business address, a professional atmosphere, phones, and other business equipment. Sometimes executive suites will even provide a shared secretary.

If you go to clients rather than having them come to you, a car or van might work as your headquarters. Keep in mind, however, that you'll have to either invest in a laptop computer or keep part of your office elsewhere.

Wherever you locate, make sure that your business does not violate zoning ordinances, rental agreements, and the community welfare. This holds true for all kinds of event planners.

Consider stockpiling space if you expect to grow quickly or store a lot of equipment so you won't have to move.

Types of Business Forms

Congratulations! You have named your business, have your DBA in hand, and you are considered the owner of a legitimate business. Now you will need to make the decision to operate as one of four business entities: a sole proprietorship, a corporation, a partnership, or a limited liability company (LLC).

Sole Proprietors

Many event planners choose to operate as sole proprietors because it's the easiest

Smart Tip

Tip...

If you opt for a home-based business, you must allocate a space that is to be used solely for your business. It could be a small area, a desk tucked into the corner of the dining room, for instance, but it must be devoted to your event planning business. It is also wise to have a separate phone line for your business. Nothing will kill your credibility faster than using your home phone line with its answering machine featuring your three-year-old singing the theme song from *Dora, The Explorer*. This is not professional. Have a separate line and a separate answering machine. This will help when tax times rolls around since your business phone expenses will be deductible. And, while on the subject of phone etiquette, never put a client on hold to speak with another client. Let your answering machine pick up any incoming calls you can't answer yourself.

type of business to form. All you have to do is file a DBA, as discussed in the sidebar on page 53, then open a business checking account in that name. You can use your personal credit card to pay for business expenditures, yet you still get tax benefits like business expense deductions. But there is a downside to the sole proprietorship. You are personally liable for any losses, bankruptcy claims, legal actions, and so on. That can wipe out both your personal and business assets if major problems arise.

Industry expert Patty Sachs operated her own business in Minneapolis as a sole proprietorship for many years and never had a problem with this legal form.

Joyce Barnes-Wolff, who owns an event planning business in Ohio, also has a sole proprietorship. "It's easy and quick," she says. "For me, this works the best." However, most banks are not eager to lend money to sole proprietorships, she points out.

General Partnership

Perhaps you are planning to work with another event planner as you form your business. Then you are forming a general partnership. Partnerships are easier to form than corporations, and you don't have to file any documents to make them legal. Each partner is responsible for the actions of the other, so it's a good idea to have a partnership agreement that is crystal clear regarding what each partner is responsible for.

Limited Liability Company

A third type of business entity is the limited liability company, or LLC, which has the tax structure of a partnership, yet protects the business owner from personal liability. This structure protects each partner's personal interests.

Corporations

The last type of business arrangement is the corporation. It is established as a totally separate legal entity from the business owner. Establishing a corporation requires filing articles of incorporation, electing officers, and holding an annual meeting. Not many event planners choose this route initially because the costs are prohibitive, and the company must pay corporate taxes. On the other hand, a corporation will find it easier to obtain financing, which would be useful if you decided to franchise your business or expand in a big way.

Although the process for creating a corporate structure is more complicated and expensive than creating other structures, it does offer protection to event planners and their assets. A corporate structure is often advantageous to a business because the corporation exists as a separate entity. It alone is legally responsible for its actions and debts. As an employee of the corporation, your personal assets are protected in most situations, even though you may own all or most of the stock. Deborah Williams and Kim Quigley turned their partnership into a C corporation on the advice of their attorney. "You could lose your home, your car, everything, with a partnership," says Williams.

According to industry expert John Daly, the decision to incorporate depends partly on how much you have at stake.

> **Bright Idea**
> Consider sharing space with a related business. For example, you could set up shop with a party supply store or a caterer. You might not only save money but also gain referrals. If you elect to share space, however, make sure you have a clear contract stating how space and responsibilities will be shared. Also, be sure to share space with a well-respected business. Sharing space with a less-than-reliable caterer will not boost your business!

In his opinion, small events are not usually a problem, but once you're doing huge events, you don't want to risk wiping out your personal assets. The main points to remember? Incorporation protects you. However, increased paperwork and taxes are disadvantages.

If deciding on a legal form for your business keeps you up at night, consider two things: First, your nails will grow back. Second, as the above examples illustrate, your business structure is not carved in stone. It can be changed.

Licenses and Permits

Most cities and counties require business operators to obtain various licenses and permits to comply with local regulations. For everyday operation of an event planning business, you may need the following:

- *Business license*: ensures proper zoning and parking
- *Vendor's permit* (varies from state to state): allows you to buy and resell
- *Health department permit*: if you also cater events and thus handle food
- *Liquor, wine, and beer licenses*: if you yourself serve alcohol
- *Sign permit*: covers size, location, and sometimes the type of sign you may use
- *County permits*: may be applicable if you are located outside city limits

Depending on the event, you may also need the following:

- *Fire Marshall permit*: for large gatherings, events with fireworks, or the display of a vehicle indoors
- *Special event permit*: if you'll be using city property
- *Street closure permit*: for closing off a street (e.g., a block party or arts festival)
- *Parade permit*: self-explanatory!

Check local regulations to see which of the above licenses and permits you'll need. But no matter where your event will take place, you may need to apply for the following types of permission:

- *Copyright permission*. The two major U.S. music-licensing companies,

Smart Tip

To find out if you need additional licenses or permits, check these sources:
- Small Business Administration, www.sba.gov
- Small Business Development Center, www.sba.gov
- Service Corps of Retired Executives, www.score.org

The Right Idea

Any original idea in a unique form can be protected under U.S. copyright. This includes cartoon characters, sculptures, paintings, plays, maps, songs, scripts, photos, books, and poems, to name but a few. There are five classes of copyrights:

1. *Class TX*: Nondramatic literary works (fiction, nonfiction, advertising copy, textbooks, etc.)

2. *Class PA*: Works of the performing arts (drama, music, choreography, etc.)

3. *Class SR*: Sound recordings (independent of musical or literary works)

4. *Class VA*: Works of the visual arts (pictures, graphics, models, maps, ads, etc.)

5. *Class RE*: Renewal registration (works originally copyrighted before January 1, 1978—all classes)

Why, you may ask, do you need to know about this? If you come up with an original logo for your service or for a type of event that you produce, you might want to copyright that logo. Similarly, you might write a script for a particular type of original event (e.g., a murder mystery/dessert party) and want to copyright it.

To apply for a copyright, send a copy of the work with an official form and a $30 application fee to the Copyright Office, Library of Congress, 101 Independence Ave. SE, Washington, DC 20559, (202) 707-3000. For more information, consult its website at www.copyright.gov.

Broadcast Music International (BMI) and the American Society of Composers, Authors, and Publishers (ASCAP), enforce their rights to collect fees. You may need copyright permission to use text materials, music, audiovisual displays, photographs, drawings, ads, drama pieces, or any number of a variety of materials. Always check for the copyright of any materials you use in an event. We do not suggest this lightly or out of a desire to "cover our act," as it were. The fact is, many artists and companies take copyright infringement very seriously. Therefore, so should you.

- *Trademark permission.* Be aware that distinctive trademarks are protected. Trademarks apply to products. For example, you may need permission to use any relevant brand names on literature you circulate about an event or about your business.

Even if your event planning business does not need a particular type of permit, always make sure that your vendors are properly licensed and have the appropriate permits.

Choosing Insurance

Knowing what kind of insurance to carry and how much to obtain is an important aspect of good risk management. Don't view insurance as an option. It is absolutely imperative that you have insurance before you plan any event.

As the owner of an event planning business, you are most likely to need the following types of insurance:

- *General liability insurance.* This is the one type of insurance you must carry, and every business owner interviewed for this book had it. Many event sites will be unavailable to you if you don't carry this coverage. General liability insurance protects a business against accidents and injuries that might occur at the event site or at your office. You may be liable for bodily injuries to customers, guests, delivery people, and other outsiders—even in cases in which you have exercised "reasonable care." As David Granger points out, "If I put down lighting and someone trips over a cord that wasn't taped down, or if one of my centerpieces catches fire, or if a stage prop falls, I need to be covered." It's a good idea to carry $1 million worth of liability insurance. In fact, Dallas planner Deborah Williams says local hotels won't do business with event planners who don't carry at least $1 million in liability insurance.

- *Workers' compensation insurance.* If you have employees, you may also want this type of insurance. Williams has it for employees at Designs Behind the Scenes. You are liable for injury to employees at work caused by problems with equipment or working conditions. In every state, an employer must insure against potential workers' comp claims. However, employee coverage and the extent of the employer's liability vary among states.

- *Auto insurance.* Cars and trucks are sources of liability. Even if you own none, you can be liable for injuries and property damage caused by employees operating their own or someone else's car while on company business.

> **Tip...**
>
> **Smart Tip**
> Some cities provide packets with explanations and all the forms you'll need for the various licenses and permits, so investigate this possibility at your town clerk's office. Also, it's a good idea to ask more than one city or county employee about the licenses you need, especially if you get information that is confusing or not what you expected.

- *Bonding.* If you sell large numbers of airline or entertainment tickets or any of several other types of goods, you may need to carry bonding. This procedure requires you to put aside money into a separate account for reimbursing clients for tickets they purchased from you in the event your business goes under. You may also need bonding to protect you if one of your employees steals or damages something at an event site. Vendors should carry their own protection. Check your state's legal requirements.

Beware!
If you operate your event planning business from your home, you may need additional coverage. Your homeowner's policy may be sufficient, but if you plan to store or use expensive machinery, such as a computer, or if customers or clients will visit your home for business purposes, you may want to purchase additional coverage. Set up an appointment with your agent to go over your insurance coverage.

Creating Effective Proposals and Agreements

To do business (and protect your company as you do it), you'll need a variety of documents. Invoices and purchase orders for an event planning business are, for the most part, the same as those for any other business. So we will concentrate our attention on proposals and several different kinds of agreements.

Proposals

Quite simply, proposals tell clients what you will do for them and at what cost. A proposal hits the high points of your creative idea(s) for the event. It is an important selling tool and might consist of any or all of the following elements:

- *History of your company.* Provide one if relevant.
- *Letters of reference.* Kudos from clients for whom you planned similar events work wonders.
- *Write-ups.* Often a complimentary newspaper or magazine article featuring your business is a valuable tool for selling your services to others. You may also want to include photographs.
- *Description of the event.* This is where you sell your ideas. Walk the client through the event, describing what guests see, hear, smell, taste, and touch. What emotions will guests feel?

- *Description of services.* This tells which vendors you'll hire and sketches out how you'll achieve what you write about in the description of the event.

- *Listing of additional services.* If you also will provide catering, floral design, or some other service, describe those services completely.

- *Production schedule.* This item lets the client know any pertinent details about the timing of the event, especially if there are critical aspects to arrange. If you're hosting a smaller event, you usually do not need this part of the proposal.

- *Event cost estimate.* This accompanies any proposal.

Make sure you include in your proposal an expiration date for the event cost estimate. You don't want to be expected to produce that event for the listed price five years from now!

> **Smart Tip** *Tip...*
>
> We've all heard it: a picture is worth a thousand words—or more! Photos in your proposal packet can make a powerful impact on prospective clients. Good photos can help to evoke a mood and a flavor, evocations that are more difficult to capture in print. Conversely, poor quality photos could kill a deal. Consider hiring a professional photographer to capture some stellar images for you or invest in a high-quality digital camera. Check Consumer Reports (www. consumerreports.org) or ask at your local camera or discount store, for advice on buying a camera. This is money well spent.

Customers must be able to visualize the event when they read your proposal. As David Granger puts it: "Proposals need to be flowery." His colleague, Deborah Williams, agrees: "Dave is phenomenal at proposals," she adds. "When you read one of his proposals, you can just see the whole thing."

You have to figure out a way to make clients visualize the event as you have designed it, and they have to understand the quality of your work. Consider including in your proposal some photos of a previous event you planned that was similar to what the client wants. Any photos included should, of course, be vivid and lively. Jaclyn Bernstein stresses the importance of asking clients a lot of questions and listening well. Catching (and using in your proposal) exact words customers have used in discussion with you helps to convey a sense of excitement about the event, she says. Enthusiasm is important, as long as your language isn't too extreme.

Agreements

The possession of signed documents detailing all aspects of the events you produce is not only helpful but also imperative to the legal health of your business.

These are descriptions of the different types of event planning agreements.

▲

- *Client agreements.* Once the client has agreed to hire your company, you need an official contract. The exact form this contract appears in will vary by state because you must conform to state code. If you draft your own client agreement, get a local attorney to take a look at it.

  We provide a sample agreement, starting on page 63, to give you an idea of elements you may want to include in your own agreement.

- *Vendor agreements.* Any vendor providing a service for your client's event

should sign a formal agreement with your planning company. As with any legal document, get your local attorney's advice. Starting on page 65 is a sample agreement with a catering company.

Make sure that any vendors you hire are properly insured and/or bonded. They must carry insurance to protect their companies (and you) from their negligence, bankruptcy, or lack of appearance at an event. Any forms of insurance or bonding that they carry should be listed in the vendor agreement (see page 65).

- *Site agreements.* Once you have selected the site that will best suit your client's needs, confirm your arrangements with the site's sales representative and ask

> **Beware!**
> Any site contract with a hotel or other lodging facility should state that if fewer rooms are occupied than expected, you will not be held responsible. Instead, attendees should be given a deadline before which they can claim a room in the reserved block at the group rate. After the deadline, any unreserved rooms are made available to the general public.

Foundation Essentials

Complete these items as you get your business started:

- ○ Develop and write a business plan
- ○ Create a powerful mission statement
- ○ Select a name for your company and apply for a DBA
- ○ Choose the best business structure for your company
- ○ Check local zoning laws to ensure that you are in compliance
- ○ Apply for the licenses and permits you will need

Sample Client Agreement

This agreement is between Right Touch Event Planning Inc. (hereafter referred to as PLANNER) and Mr. John Doe (hereafter referred to as CLIENT).

I. *PLANNER agrees to provide:*

- ○ Research, design, organization, coordination, and evaluation of the CLIENT's Silver Wedding Anniversary
- ○ A social event to begin at 8:00 P.M. on Saturday, May 23, 20xx, at the CLIENT's residence and to end by 2:00 A.M. the following day
- ○ Comprehensive general liability insurance to cover damage caused by any action, or inaction, of the PLANNER or of any individuals contracted by the PLANNER
- ○ Vendors as agreed upon with the CLIENT (see attachment)
- ○ Additional staffing for the event

II. *CLIENT agrees to provide:*

- ○ The CLIENT's residence as site for the event
- ○ The CLIENT's kitchen and equipment therein for use by the caterers and bar staff
- ○ One individual to serve as decision maker for the PLANNER
- ○ Decisions in a timely manner
- ○ Homeowners' insurance to cover damage caused by an act of God or by any action, or inaction, of the CLIENT or of the CLIENT's guests

III. *FEES*

The PLANNER will receive a commission amounting to 15 percent of the total event cost. The total event cost is not to exceed $10,000.

IV. *TERMS*

The CLIENT agrees to provide payment for the services described. This payment shall be remitted to the PLANNER according to the following schedule: Upon signing of this document:

- ○ 50 percent of total event cost, based on estimate
- ○ 25 percent of commission, based on estimated event cost

Sample Client Agreement, continued

May 24, 20xx:

○ Remainder of final event cost

○ Remainder of commission, based on final event cost

V. *CANCELLATION*

Should the PLANNER cancel his or her services for any reason other than acts of God, the CLIENT shall receive a refund of all pre-paid fees, less any expenses incurred on behalf of the event. Should the CLIENT cancel the event, the following payments shall be due:

○ Cancellation more than 60 days before event: 25 percent of estimated event cost and 50 percent of commission

○ Cancellation between 15 and 60 days (incl.) before event: 75 percent of estimated event cost and 50 percent of commission

○ Cancellation less than 15 days before event: 100 percent of estimated event cost and 75 percent of commission

VI. *FORCE MAJEURE*

This agreement is automatically canceled if the event is interrupted by an act of God, by war, or by strikes.

VII. *HOLD HARMLESS and INDEMNIFICATION*

The PLANNER and CLIENT agree to hold one another harmless from negligence and to mutually indemnify.

VIII. *ACCEPTANCE OF FULL AGREEMENT*

This agreement, plus attachments, constitutes the full agreement. Any changes to this agreement must be approved in writing by both PLANNER and CLIENT. Those parties affixing signatures below agree to accept the terms and conditions of this agreement.

_____   _____

Client   *Date*

_____   _____

Planner   *Date*

Sample Vendor Agreement

This agreement is between Right Touch Event Planning Inc. (hereafter referred to as PLANNER) and Sweetness and Light Catering Inc. (hereafter referred to as VENDOR).

> EVENT DATE: May 23, 20xx
> EVENT ARRIVAL TIME: 7:00 P.M.
> EVENT START TIME: 8:00 P.M.
> EVENT STOP TIME: 2:00 A.M. May 24

I. *VENDOR agrees to provide:*
- ○ Ten trays of hors d'oeuvres, as detailed in attachment
- ○ Buffet dinner for 40 persons, as detailed in attachment
- ○ Dessert buffet, as detailed in attachment
- ○ All serving equipment, including, but not limited to: trays, tongs, chafing dishes, and buffet ranges
- ○ Serving staff, as detailed in attachment
- ○ Cleanup crew, as detailed in attachment
- ○ Proof of insurance

II. *PLANNER agrees to provide:*
- ○ Complimentary parking for VENDOR and staff
- ○ Utilities (gas, electricity, water)
- ○ Kitchen facilities
- ○ Tables and table linens
- ○ One individual on-site to act as liaison with vendor
- ○ Liability insurance for the event

III. *FEES*

PLANNER shall provide the following payment to VENDOR:

Hor d'oeuvres	$300
Buffet dinner (40 persons)	$600
Dessert buffet	$450
Serving and cleanup	$180
Subtotal:	$1,530
Less referral fee	−$80
Total:	*$1,450*

Sample Vendor Agreement, continued

IV. *TERMS*

PLANNER shall pay VENDOR a deposit of 50 percent ($725) upon execution of agreement. Balance due by June 23, 200x.

V. *CANCELLATION*

If the VENDOR cancels for any reason, he or she shall forfeit all funds received or due and shall repay PLANNER any funds advanced for this event. If the PLANNER cancels for any reason, he or she must provide the following payments to VENDOR:

○ Cancellation more than 60 days before event: Refund of referral fee ($80)

○ Cancellation between 15 and 60 days (incl.) before event: 25 percent of total fee

○ Cancellation less than 15 days before event: 75 percent of total fee

VI. *FORCE MAJEURE*

This agreement is automatically canceled if the event is interrupted by an act of God, by war, or by strikes.

VII. *HOLD HARMLESS and INDEMNIFICATION*

The PLANNER and CLIENT agree to hold one another harmless from negligence and to mutually indemnify.

VIII. *ACCEPTANCE OF FULL AGREEMENT*

This agreement, plus attachments, constitutes the full agreement. Any changes to this agreement must be approved in writing by both PLANNER and CLIENT. Those parties affixing signatures below agree to accept the terms and conditions of this agreement.

_____   _____

Client   *Date*

_____   _____

Planner   *Date* for a written contract or letter of agreement. Review the contract carefully and clarify any misunderstandings or ambiguities with the site representative. The contract should include the arrangements for guest rooms and any activities scheduled to take place at the site. Contracts should also include the site's cancellation and deposit policies.

Now that you have begun building a strong foundation for your business, in Chapter 5 we will move on to financing your business.

Financing Your Business

The axiom tells us that we have to spend money to make money, and, of course, this holds true in developing an event planning business. The good news, though, is that you can launch a successful business with a shoestring budget. Perhaps you envision planning five events during your first year in business and using space in your home as your work site. This business model is relatively inexpensive to create and highly viable. Conversely, if you are planning to launch a full-time event planning business, then the startup costs will be considerably higher. This flexibility—part time vs. full time—makes event planning a terrific career opportunity for many types, from stay-at-home moms hoping to earn a few thousand dollars per year to new college graduates planning to create full-scale businesses generating full-time pay and benefits.

> **Stat Fact**
> According to several online sources, trends in kids' birthday parties continue to focus on creativity and interesting, interactive venues like museums and zoos. Also, kids' parties have become so unique and fun, parents are lingering—focus on planning family-oriented birthday parties and you may have your schedule full! Creativity doesn't add a thing to your startup costs!

The First Step

Remember, first things first. Start by estimating your business expenditures over the startup period and over the first six months of operation (see Business Expenses Worksheet on page 72). Take your figures from the "My Own" column in the Startup Expenses Worksheet on page 21 in Chapter 2 and put these figures in the "Startup" column. If you have not yet made those estimates, now is the time to do so.

First, work horizontally. Add the "Startup" figures and the "First Six Months" figures to produce the "Total Cost" figures for each row. Then, working vertically, add up the "Total Cost" figures. The "Total Required" figure is the approximate amount you will need to start the business and keep it running for six months.

Note that this business expense worksheet includes no costs for planning particular events. You will incur these costs even if you plan no events at all. In that sense, then, these are all fixed costs. When you contract to plan an event, you should receive a deposit from each client to cover some of the immediate costs associated with producing that event (e.g., vendor deposits). The price you charge a client for planning an event will cover not only your costs for that event but also some fraction of your fixed costs.

> **Beware!**
> Do not underestimate your communications budget. If you have multiple phone lines, a cellular phone, a pager, internet access, etc., these are ongoing expenses. Joyce Barnes-Wolff estimates her monthly communications costs to be her second largest expense, after labor.

In Chapter 10, which deals with financial management, we'll discuss how to price your planning services and how to figure out a break-even point for your business.

For now, you need an approximate idea of how much money you'll require for your business and your own living expenses until your company makes a profit. Again, this is a highly personal point. Perhaps you are recently retired and want to launch a small-scale business. In other words, this will not be a primary income source. For others, their event planning businesses will be their primary income source. Making this determination greatly affects startup costs. The recent retiree will spend substantially less on startup costs than the person envisioning event planning as a full-time occupation.

Each company's break-even point will be different. Connecticut planner Lauren Polastri's company, The Other Woman, was profitable within the first year, in part due to low startup costs. New York City planner Jaclyn Bernstein bought an existing business, and her company was profitable within six months. Event planner Joyce Barnes-Wolff made a small profit in her business's first year. It was enough to pay herself a salary but not enough to reinvest in the company.

Once you have an idea of your capital requirements, it is time to think about your financing options.

Finding Financing

To find your best source of financing, look in the mirror. Most entrepreneurs invest their own resources first, and so should you. Your own capital is immediately available, carries no interest obligation, and requires no surrender of business equity. Event planner Martin Van Keken used money from the sale of another business. Nearly all entrepreneurs we interviewed used at least some of their own money.

If you do not have the cash reserves to launch your business, consider these sources:

- *Friends and relatives.* If you opt to turn to friends and relatives, do so with extreme care. You don't want to sour a lifelong relationship by creating a financial misunderstanding with a close friend or family member. If you choose to make a financial arrangement with a friend or relative, then absolutely enlist the help of an attorney to create a contract, stipulating your obligations as well as your understanding of the transaction. Is the money a loan or a gift? Will the lender receive a percentage of the profits? Make sure that all parties understand the transaction.

Smart Tip

Tip...

If you choose to finance your business using credit cards, call around for the best rates. Often, if you call and speak to a representative from your credit card company, you can negotiate a better rate than the one advertised.

Business Expenses Worksheet

	Startup	First Six Months	Total Cost
Rent/deposit			
Equipment			
Inventory			
Licenses and taxes			
Phone/utilities			
Payroll			
Advertising/promotion			
Legal fees and accounting			
Insurance			
Vehicle maintenance/mileage			
Misc. (postage, signage, office supplies, etc.)			
Total required			

- *Credit cards.* Again, proceed with extreme caution if you opt to use credit cards to finance your new business. Interest on credit cards can be crippling and could easily erase any profits you might make.
- *Equity.* Some business owners choose to draw on lines of equity, perhaps a home equity line. Remember, though, this is not free money. Even when interest rates are low on these lines of credit, you still will have incurred additional debt. Proceed carefully and consider interest payments when you plot your financial growth.
- *Venture capital.* This is private equity, typically provided by outside vendors. Venture capitalists tend to invest in higher risk businesses that have the potential for above-average returns. Most event planners will not rely on venture capital.
- *Banks.* You will be able to use your business plan to approach banks for loans, many geared specifically toward those creating a small business. It is imperative, when you approach a bank, that your business plan is thoughtful and thorough. Also, local banks are often more interested in financing small local businesses than larger, non-local chains.

- *Small Business Association*. Contact the SBA (www.sba.gov) for information about financing your developing small business.

If there is any single piece of advice most appropriate for the new entrepreneur in need of money, it is to make a careful assessment of the proposed value of the business, the amount of capital needed to finance it, in what increments it is needed, and the period of time you'll need the capital for. You'll need a business plan. You have made one, right? If not, go back to Chapter 2. (Do not pass GO. Do not collect $200. However, a good plan will help you collect a great deal more than that.)

Once you have your startup money, it's time to go shopping for equipment.

Buying Equipment and Inventory

You'll need equipment and inventory for your company. In this section we'll discuss the must-haves and the nice-to-haves for event planners.

Before you go out and spend thousands of dollars, make a list, check it twice, and trim it well. Industry expert and author Patty Sachs advises new owners of event planning businesses to keep startup costs low by buying only the minimum equipment and supplies. You need basic equipment, letterhead, business cards, a computer bookkeeping program, license or permit fees, internet service, and brochures or fliers to get you started. You will also need insurance, but you should not need inventory (e.g., party supplies). Lauren Polastri rents the party supplies she needs. And, says Kim Quigley, "We bought on an as-used basis."

Essential Equipment

Most event planners use standard office equipment such as desks, computers, and a printer/scanner/copier/fax. Many planners use meeting management software designed specifically for their field.

Small event planning businesses may not require much equipment. But no matter what the size of your business, invest in the following must-haves:

- *Vehicle*. You can use your own car, but you will need a vehicle for visiting clients and traveling to and from

Smart Tip

Before getting caught up in the latest technology just because it is available, consider what benefit it will provide your business. For example, while the iPad is a fun gadget, it has become popular with planners for things like easy seating arrangement reconfiguring and apps that keep you on schedule.

event sites. Using your own car will reduce the amount of startup capital you need. Other options are to lease or purchase a company vehicle. Remember, your car is a reflection of you and your business. Keep it tidy. Don't leave your brochures and paperwork strewn about.

- *Office furniture*. Good quality used furniture may be an option. You'll need a desk, chair, filing cabinets, and bookshelves. In fact, you may already own most of this equipment.

- *Cellular phone or pagers*. Cell phones have become an indispensable part of doing business in the event planning industry. Some entrepreneurs use a pager and cell phone together to save money. Make sure to buy a headset. Many states now mandate hands-free phone use while driving.

Smart Tip

Be creative about your office location. As a startup, you can use a home office and see potential clients at their space or perhaps at the venue location for their event. When you are ready to lease a space, work with a landlord who will reward you for being a great tenant. Likewise, utilize other vendors—insurers, for example—who will reward your loyalty and provide you with great rates.

- *Multiple phone lines*. One phone line is usually not enough. Install a multiline (push-button) phone system, allowing you to switch back and forth between lines while on one phone. In general, you'll need one phone line for every five employees (if you have any, that is). It is ideal to keep your work line and personal line separate to appear professional to prospective clients. Having separate phone lines will help at tax time, as well, when it is time to deduct expenses.

- *Answering machine or voice mail*. You must provide a way for clients, vendors, and others to leave messages in your absence. Consider using music on your answering machine that reflects the tone of your business. These little touches add to your professional image. Don't rely on a computerized standard message for your voice mail—potential clients want to hear a human voice announcing your personal business when they get your message. Otherwise, they are likely to hang up and call the next event planner on their list of prospects.

- *Computer*. A computer is essential not only for producing professional-looking proposals, but also for keeping records and tracking information. It is a valuable time-saver to be able to pull up a proposal for a previous event, make the necessary adjustments, and then send the revised proposal to the new client. A computer is also necessary for using the internet, a valuable tool for event planners. See Chapters 8 and 9 on websites and social media for more on the value of computers for today's business.

- *E-mail and internet access.* E-mail and internet access are vital to your business. You'll be able to find vendors, research hotels and convention sites, network with other event planners and more in a quick and inexpensive fashion using your internet access. You will also be able to do market research as well as market your business. In other words, e-mail and internet access are absolutely indispensable.

- *Printer.* The ability to send out professional-looking proposals is important, and you'll need a printer to do that. Unless your business does very high-end events, you won't need to go to the expense of a laser printer; a good inkjet printer should be fine.
- *Digital camera.* The ability to show clients your work online can be valuable. Digital cameras carry a wide price range, from $150 to $550. Get the best quality you can afford—even the new digital SLRs, which have a viewfinder like the camera of yesteryear, are lightweight and very portable.

What Computer Do You Need?

There is no question you will need a computer, but exactly what you need will depend on your business size and type of event planning you do.

- ○ *Laptop.* For many event planners, a laptop computer is as much computer as you need. Laptops and netbooks (a tad smaller version of a laptop) now have significant memory and processing power to do just about everything you need to do. And it's portable, so you can take it with you on site and to visit clients and still have everything you need right at your fingertips.
- ○ *Desktop.* If you work at your desk a lot, a desktop computer can be a good tool with a netbook, tablet, or small laptop/notebook computer as an adjunct, in-the-field tool. If your business requires you to download lots of high-res photography or review DVDs, the desktop will give you the power and peripherals that a netbook typically doesn't, such as a DVD drive. And the setup for a desktop tends to be much more efficient, capable of accommodating large-screen monitors and ergonomic keyboards.

- *Software.* Virus-detection software, as described earlier, is a necessity, and you must update it regularly.

There are five main types of software you may need: a word-processing program, a spreadsheet program, a relational database, desktop publishing software, and specialty software. Here are a few examples. For more information about software, consult the websites provided in our Appendix.

1. *Word processing program.* This allows you to write text. Used for writing evaluations, forms, letters, lists, and anything else you want to write. Most planners we spoke to use Microsoft Word. Make sure you have a recent version (approximately $200).

2. *Spreadsheet program.* Helps you manipulate numbers. Used for producing outlines, schedules, timelines, budgets, and calendars, among other uses. Excel (about $200) is often cited by event planners, as is Quicken. The latter costs anywhere from $40, for the most basic version, to $60 for a more luxurious version.

3. *Relational database.* Allows you to manage, update, and use information from other databases. Used to produce name badges, receipts, reports, tickets, etc. If you are planning only small events, you may not need this type of software. If you choose to buy meeting management software, you will want to do some research. Ask other planners what type of software they use. With hundreds of varieties of software on the market—with price points ranging from $100 to thousands of dollars—you will have to determine which software works best for your company and best services the types of events you plan. For complete reports on software products for the meeting industry, check out Corbin Ball's website, at www.corbinball.com/tipstools for his reports and reviews on Meetings Technology Software Tools. This guide details each software's strengths as weaknesses as well as offering price information.

4. *Desktop publishing.* Gives your products a polished look. Used for name badges, posters, press releases, signage, tickets, etc. Microsoft Publisher ($150) is a good starting point.

Tip...

Smart Tip

Make developing a company logo a priority. Part of creating a business is about developing a brand image. We all recognize McDonald's golden arches and Nike's swoosh. Although design software, such as InDesign, makes it possible for a novice to create a logo, it is often better to pay a graphic designer for this service. You want your logo to be professional, memorable, and unique. Don't opt for a clip art logo. These can look tacky and may show up on another planner's marketing materials. Finally, make sure your logo appears on everything, from your business cards to your website.

5. *Specialty software.* This type of software will allow you to perform specific tasks. Used for name badges, place cards, signage, tickets, diagrams, floor plans, etc. For example, room design software lets you design floor plans for meetings. Once you enter the room's dimensions, you can place elements such as walls, doors, and seats in various arrangements until you reach the best one for your event. You may find that all your specialty software needs are met through your other software, such as your meeting management software. As a new business developer, you probably do not need to worry too much about buying specialty software. As your company grows and you determine a need for this software, then make a decision to buy.

Smart Tip

Tip...

Create a database of all your vendor information, including products/services, prices, policies, and delivery times. By having this information computerized and retrievable within seconds, you will drastically reduce your time and work. Back up this data on your computer or on a disc and make sure you also have a Rolodex or some other hard copy of the list, in the event of a computer failure.

Some event planners keep a collection of decorative items like these candy jars and rent them to clients. *Photo courtesy of SignatureEventsNH.*

▲

There are many other items you might need. If you have a larger business, some of the following equipment items may be necessities. For smaller companies, these may fall into the nice-to-have category.

- *Walkie-talkies.* Jaclyn Bernstein and her employees often use walkie-talkies to communicate on the job. You can buy a basic walkie-talkie for $40; a high-end one will cost $150.

- *Laminating machine.* Bernstein also has a laminating machine to make signage for the events her business produces. Cost of this equipment ranges from $50 to $250.

Profile

Jaclyn Bernstein frequently gives thank-you gifts to clients. These range from the relatively small (e.g., a New York cheesecake, a T-shirt, or cookies in the form of New York taxi cabs) to the more costly (e.g., a crystal apple). All are designed to remind the client of her midtown Manhattan business. "Showing appreciation and making the client feel special are important parts of doing business," she says.

- *Typewriter.* Handy for filling out forms, a typewriter may also help you out of a temporary computer emergency.

- *Copier.* If your company makes more than a few hundred copies per month or if you don't have time to keep running out for copies, you should consider investing in a copier to save time spent going to the copy shop. For $300 to $500, you can buy a multifunction machine that combines the functions of printer/copier/fax machine. Or, for a photocopier that can really perform, consider leasing.

- *Scanner.* This piece of equipment is occasionally handy to have, but it's not essential for event planners. If you don't already have one, you're probably better off buying a digital camera so you can avoid scanning your photos into your website. If you do buy a scanner, you'll note a large quality/price range. The simplest scanner costs about $50, and the most deluxe one, capable of scanning not only documents and large stacks of photos but also slides and negatives, is about $300. Some printers come equipped with scanners as well as copying capabilities.

- *Fax machine.* Most entrepreneurs benefit from being able to fax documents to clients. You will probably be able to fax from your computer, scanning documents first then using eFax or some other faxing software.

Tracking Inventory

Some planners store an inventory of decorations and props. However, most rent these as needed, especially large items like gazebos and arches. You must consider both the storage space requirements and the maintenance requirements of inventory, as both will affect your overhead costs. Remember, unless you store only very small, low-maintenance items, you'll need more space and employee (or your own) time devoted to inventory upkeep. And no matter what kind of inventory you stock, you'll have to spend time tracking it.

How many smaller inventory items (e.g., centerpiece items, candles, etc.) should you stock? That depends in large part on whether you handle event décor yourself or contract it out to a designer or decorator. Most of the event planners we talked to hire vendors to provide décor. Therefore, they stock very little inventory. And so should you, at least at the beginning. As a rule, you should buy items as you need them. Most planners we talked to had no startup inventory costs at all.

So what do planners routinely keep as inventory? Those we interviewed listed the following items:

- *Photos and videos*. Most planners keep photos of events their companies have produced. This industry is a very visual one. "People want to see what you've done," says David Granger. Many planners put photos on their websites as well as use them in portfolios and keep them in resource cabinets. Photos are also vital when producing proposals to present to clients.

- *Vendor catalogs and brochures*. Joyce Barnes-Wolff has several resource cabinets filled with these. Well-chosen catalogs and brochures are a good source of ideas and valuable reference aids for unusual items.

- *Gifts*. Several planners stock gifts for clients. Jaclyn Bernstein keeps a variety. Martin Van Keken stocks gifts of silver-plated yo-yos with the company logo.

- *Fabric*. Fabric accounts for most of Martin Van Keken's inventory. He has an extensive collection, upon which he relies heavily. David Granger keeps three-ring binders of linen swatches. Some planners, like Jaclyn Bernstein, own table linens.

- *Floral containers*. Most planners keep containers for floral arrangements. These include urns, wrought-iron stands, and bowls for floating arrangements, besides the more traditional vases. Williams, Quigley, and Granger rent plants and other items as part of their business. Their table-top décor ranges from statuary items to antique hat boxes. If you use a florist or greenhouse, however, your floral-container needs will be minimal.

Dollar Stretcher

If you do choose to buy props for your business, keep an eye on the discount stores, particularly for post-holiday sales. Stock up after Valentine's day for Valentine's props—some discounted as much as 90 percent. Then when Cupid's holiday rolls around the following year, you will have low-cost props for a Valentine-themed party.

- *Lighting.* Most planners either rent lights or hire a lighting company. And they buy candles for specific events.

Our suggestion about equipment also holds true for inventory: Buy only what you need to get started. Most items should be acquired on a per-event basis. To make sure you are ready to start up, fill in the checklist below.

Once you have bought the required equipment, inventory, and other supplies for your event planning business, it's time to consider hiring the help you'll need.

Beware!
Don't forget less obvious costs. These can include, but are not restricted to, items such as the following: association memberships, subscriptions to industry publications, professional photography services, small promotional gifts, a new-business open house, custom colors for special print pieces, professional portfolio creation, van rental for transporting larger equipment, and T-shirts or uniforms for your hired helpers for larger events.

Startup Checklist

Equipment
- ❏ Vehicle
- ❏ Office furniture
- ❏ Phone
- ❏ Phone line(s)
- ❏ Answering machine or voice mail
- ❏ Cellular phone/pager
- ❏ Computer
- ❏ Printer
- ❏ Scanner
- ❏ Digital camera
- ❏ Software (general)
- ❏ Software (event planning)
- ❏ E-mail/internet access
- ❏ Website

- ❏ Fax machine
- ❏ Copier
- ❏ Typewriter
- ❏ Laminating machine
- ❏ Walkie-talkies

Inventory/Miscellaneous
- ❏ Vendor catalogs
- ❏ Client gifts
- ❏ Fabric
- ❏ Floral containers
- ❏ Lighting
- ❏ Miscellaneous (office supplies)
- ❏ Miscellaneous (write in)

Hiring Employees and Outside Vendors

Even if you plan to develop an event planning business focusing primarily on small social events, you will still find it necessary, at times, to hire help. You will likely want to hire temporary employees to help with specific events. Larger event planners will opt to hire permanent employees.

Choosing employees—whether temporary or permanent—can be a deal maker, or breaker, for your growing company. You need a reliable team around you.

The planners we interviewed for this guide had anywhere from 0 to 12 permanent employees. Lauren Polastri hires temporary help as necessary. Because she lives in an area near the shore, her business booms during summer months. During these busy times, she takes on temporary employees.

Deborah Williams and Kim Quigley did not hire any permanent employees for the first three years. Their company now has 11, counting themselves. Joyce Barnes-Wolff, however, prefers a smaller company, with only herself and an assistant as permanent employees.

All planners—even those with permanent staffs in place—hire temporary personnel, often in large numbers, on an as-needed basis. As is the case for Lauren Polastri, you might live in an area with well-defined on- and off-seasons. If this is the case, then you will need to hire staff during busy or peak times. Part-time employees may help set up and tear down an event site. They might also be servers or ushers. Part-time workers are ideal for office tasks such as entering data into the computer and addressing and mailing envelopes.

Someone, whether yourself, a permanent staff member, or a temporary employee, will be needed to fill each of the following roles:

- *Office manager*: oversees and coordinates employees and may also handle administrative, clerical, and office-supply duties
- *Planner*: helps plan events
- *Sales staff*: sells events to clients; networks to gain additional business
- *Designer*: handles décor if you do not hire vendors to do that
- *Public relations representative*: handles public relations involving clients, vendors, suppliers, and the general public
- *Director of marketing*: takes charge of advertising and promotion; often, the public relations representative

Smart Tip

When hiring employees, consider the types of benefits you will be able to offer. These are an important incentive when choosing employees, as you will tend to field a better applicant pool if you offer benefits, including paid vacation, sick days, personal days, flexible work schedules, trips to professional conferences, company-funded professional training, and health insurance, for instance. Joyce Barnes-Wolff joined the local chamber of commerce to provide benefits for her employees. "I needed insurance I could not afford on an individual basis," she says. "It's more affordable as a member." Benefits come at a price, though. Full-time employees will cost you between 15 percent and 30 percent above their wages or salaries, depending on the benefits you offer.

and the director of marketing are the same person

- *Bookkeeper*: tracks all business and per-event expenses, and may also prepare tax returns; if you hire an accountant to do these tasks, you may not need a bookkeeper
- *On-site assistant*: helps set up and tear down at the event site
- *Setup staff*: greets guests, helps run registration or concession stands, serves food and/or drinks
- *Craft services staff*: provides help with craft items, preparation of invitations, etc.
- *Kitchen staff*: cleans up
- *Gofer*: runs errands
- *Driver*: delivers supplies to the venue

Smart Tip

If you are planning a golden (50th) or more anniversary event, the celebrants are entitled to a note from the current U.S. President. Simply e-mail the White House at www.comments@whitehouse.gov. Do this at least six weeks in advance, although the more lead time you give, the more likely the note will be received in time for the event.

Note that the above list is about roles, not titles. There is considerable variety in titles given to employees, but whether you use informal titles or more formal ones (e.g., production coordinator, account manager, operations assistant), the tasks are the same.

Tell It Like It Is

When you decide it is time to hire employees, write a clear and detailed job description that outlines the objectives of the job (while you're at it, write your own job description—this will help you to delegate and assign job descriptions to others). Use bulleted points to target the responsibilities of the position, the working conditions, and the relationships of the position to other jobs. Also clearly delineate the ideal candidate's skill set. This is critical because when you interview prospective candidates, these will act as a type of checklist. It is tempting to hire employees that you immediately like, but do not necessarily have the strongest skills. Try not to let emotion take over when hiring employees. Of course, it is important that you and your employees' working styles mesh. As New York City planner Jaclyn Bernstein puts it, "You have to be friends when you work crazy hours with these people." Remember, too, to hire qualified candidates.

Don't be alarmed by the length of this list. You do not need to hire a separate employee for each of these duties. Rather, you may choose to fulfill all or most of these duties yourself.

Reaching Out to Candidates

Once you have determined the type of positions you need to fill, you will need to advertise these open positions. Don't skimp on this step. Simply put, you want to cast your net as widely as possible to garner the best employees.

Advertising

Consider placing an advertisement in your local and regional newspapers. If the job you are filling is a more senior-level position, then also consider advertisements in larger newspapers as well as trade journals. These national ads, though, will be much more expensive, so plan on placing national ads only when the position warrants. Employment ads are typically placed in the classified section. Call your local paper and ask for an advertising representative who can walk you through the options. You may choose a simple three-line ad, or select a splashier, larger ad with a border helping to draw readers' attention. Be specific about your needs: hours, responsibilities, pay range, benefits, and qualities the applicant must possess (e.g., previous event planning experience). Finally, make sure no words are misspelled in this ad. Sounds simple, but, too often, classified ads make their way into print filled with typos. This will make you look less than professional. Run spell check and make sure everything is in tip-top spelling shape.

- *Online newspaper advertising.* Check with the advertising representative at your local paper to see if the newspaper offers an online option. Most newspapers offer packages, including print only, online only, or both types of advertising. If the newspaper offers an online option, plan on placing an online as well as print version of your advertisement.

- *Online job sites.* Online employment advertising on sites such as www.Craigslist.org and www.Monster.com is booming with more and more event planners turning to it to find employees. However, you really are pulling in a national audience—make it clear in your ad where the job is located to weed out far-flung candidates who will likely not be moving 1,500 miles to take the job you have to offer paying $14 per hour.

- *Colleges and universities.* Colleges and universities often have their own newspapers as well as websites on which you can post your job openings. This is an excellent source for finding able candidates, especially for less senior positions.
- *Word of mouth.* Like so many other aspects of the event planning industry, word of mouth often proves invaluable in finding key employees. Let your vendors and other event planners know that you are looking for employees. Get the word out

Beware!
Although it might be tempting to take up your mother's offer to help staff your growing business, these arrangements too often end in misunderstandings, with mom, perhaps, feeling she is underappreciated. If you do choose to work with friends or family, treat this as a professional arrangement and pay them as you would other employees.

and you will start hearing about candidates who might be suitable for your company.

Interviewing Applicants

As you begin hearing from prospective applicants, you will want to read through their resumes and create a point system, perhaps from 1 to 10, giving 1's to unqualified candidates and 10's to top candidates. You shouldn't have many 1's (if you wrote an apt job description, unqualified applicants aren't likely to apply) nor 10's (dream candidates are, as the name implies, rare). As you survey the resumes, use your rating system to decide which applicants to interview.

Interviewing Strategies

Plan on interviewing five to ten applicants for more senior positions, fewer for less senior spots. When an applicant arrives for an interview, have her complete an application form. These are available at local business supply stores such as Staples. You'll want to ask all candidates the same series of questions, ensuring a fair process. For help in formulating these questions, check www.job-interview.net. This site offers tips and advice about job interviewing and appropriate questions.

Take notes during interviews so you can review your notes later and winnow these candidates to two finalists. Ask these two for a second interview. Again, ensure fairness by asking both candidates the same series of questions. Take notes so you can access responses of both candidates after the interviews and make a final selection.

After the second interview, you will need to write an offer letter to the winning candidate, laying out your proposal, complete with pay structure and benefits. Once you and the applicant have signed the letter, you should let the other finalist know that the position is filled. Wait until the winning applicant has formally accepted before letting the losing candidate know the bad news. Too many times, the winning candidate has to decline the offer. Perhaps she received another offer and is unable to take the job. If this is the case, you will need to turn to your second candidate.

Always keep all candidates apprised of your time frame for hiring and let them know when to expect news. Always follow through, including making the tough calls, letting candidates know when they aren't selected.

Paying Your Employees

There are many variables to consider when paying your staff. For instance, in more urban areas of the country, pay tends to be higher. Compensation is also based on the employee's experience level and amount of responsibility. An inexperienced worker with only moderate responsibility makes anywhere from $18,000 to $32,000. An experienced employee with heavy responsibility probably makes between $25,000 and $45,000.

If you hire temporary help in coordinating an event, industry expert Patty Sachs says, the average wage is $10 to $15 per hour for setup staff. Craft service staff make $8 to $10 per hour.

You can pay other temporary or part-time employees either hourly or per event. They usually earn $8 to $10 per hour. If you decide to pay your intern (which will make attracting one easier), consider an hourly wage between $8 and $10 per hour or offering a stipend, i.e., a flat amount compensating the intern for a specific amount of time, usually for the duration of the semester. Stipends can range from $500 to $1,000 per semester. If your intern is a graduate student trained in some facet of event planning, you should expect to pay anywhere from $12 to $15 per hour, depending on responsibilities and, again, on the area of the country. If you live in an urban area where teenage baby sitters command $15 an hour, then you can count on paying your hourly staffers a higher-than-average hourly stipend.

Bright Idea

If a local college offers courses in event management or related areas (e.g., travel and tourism, hotel management), part-time employees and interns should be easy to find. Contact the head of the department and ask about the internship program. Local chapters of industry associations such as ISES and MPI may also offer internship referrals. And you can look on the web (see the Appendix).

Training Time

Be a good boss and take the time to adequately train your new hires. There is simply nothing more frustrating for a new employee than being left to flounder. Spend the time needed to train your new hires and they will quickly get up to speed. Plan on providing each employee with a detailed job description, delineating his or her responsibilities. Clarity and open lines of communication are key factors when dealing with employees.

Museums make dramatic event venues, such as this one at the Currier Museum in Manchester, New Hampshire. *Photo courtesy of SignatureEventsNH.*

Choosing Vendors

At the heart of a successful event planner's business is a team of reliable vendors. It can't be overstated: Your events will be marred by even one bad vendor. Just as a bad apple ruins the lot, one bad vendor may leave a bad image in your client's mind of the event as a whole. Perhaps the florist arrives with wilted and faded centerpieces. It's hard to erase this image from the minds of both your client and attendees. You must do your due diligence when it comes to finding top-rate vendors.

Types of Vendors

- *Art director*: handles design, computer imaging, etc.
- *Caterer/bartender*: serves food and beverages
- *Calligrapher*: handles lettering on invitations and signage
- *Decorator*: provides décor

▲

- *Florist*: provides floral arrangements
- *Graphic artist*: designs and executes event posters or invitations
- *Photographer/videographer*: photographs, records, and preserves the event
- *Performer*: provides entertainment
- *Transportation/parking personnel*: drives and parks vehicles

Finding the A-List Suppliers

As outlined above, even if a mistake is a vendor's fault, the mishap will reflect on you because you are managing the event. That's what makes researching vendors so important. David Granger picks his with extreme care. "Choosing vendors means knowing them and trusting them," he says. As do most event planners, Jaclyn Bernstein makes her choices with long-term relationships in mind. She has even had business come her way through vendors who know her.

> **Bright Idea**
>
> Remember, you are working in a "fun" industry that often involves celebration. Consider a weekly or monthly office celebration. Bring in something simple, like cookies or doughnuts. Anything of this nature improves office morale. Consider a monthly themed celebration. These events don't need to be fancy. A themed breakfast could be as simple as providing pirate hats, eye patches, and doughnuts for a festive *Pirates of the Caribbean* morning kick-off.
>
> If you want a good motto to do business by, consider one of author and industry consultant Patty Sachs': "Don't wait—celebrate!"

> **Beware!**
>
> Before you hire any vendors, make sure they carry the proper insurance (see Chapter 4) and meet any other legal requirements. A valet-parking service, for instance, needs to be insured, and perhaps bonded, in case a valet damages a car while he or she parks it. A caterer needs a food-handling permit and insurance. Even entertainers may need to carry insurance.

Joyce Barnes-Wolff has "the best Rolodex in the Midwest," she says. So she knows who's right for an event. "I can pull in the best people from across the area."

All the event planners interviewed for this book cautioned against letting your fingers do the walking when it comes to finding the best vendors. The best idea, successful event planners say, is to ask questions and listen carefully to the answers. Ask other event planners and clients about their experiences with vendors. The names of the best—and worst—vendors will be mentioned again and again. Keep a list of both those that are recommended and those with tarnished

Inside Out

In their book, *The Art of Event Design* (Primedia Business Magazines & Media Inc.), authors Liese Gardner and Susan Terpening point out several benefits of working with individuals from outside the special events industry. The following are good ways to add style and distinction to the events you plan; such a strategy can also be a money saver. Consider the following possibilities:

○ *Art students.* You can end up with interesting and inexpensive centerpieces if you get art students to make them for you. Check out the art department at the nearest college or university. Also take a look at the theater department if you need costumes or a backdrop for an event. Sometimes rentals are possible.

○ *Art dealers.* See if you can rent paintings for an event.

○ *Music students.* Need a pianist for an event? Consider the nearest school of music. Many students studying for master's degrees or doctorates will perform for a fraction of the cost of hiring a professional.

○ *Window dressers.* Go window shopping and find out who designed the displays you admire. That individual may make an excellent décor consultant for you.

These are only a few of many possibilities. Use your imagination! But because these individuals may not have their own insurance, make sure you have coverage for anyone on-site during the event.

reputations. With these lists in hand, start researching the vendors on your A-list, recording the following information:

- Vendor name, address, contact information
- Area of service
- Prices
- Lead times required
- Payment policy
- Refund policy
- Discounts offered
- Specialty items/services

▲

- Insurance coverage
- Types of licenses and permits held

This vendor file is extremely important because it can save you hours of research time down the road, Sachs says. By having all this information right at your fingertips, you'll be able to conduct your vendor searches more effectively. Keep building this file as each new event comes along. A computerized file can be even more of a time saver.

Before you hire a vendor for the first time, find out all you can about the company's history. Ask for letters of reference, too. Or, ask if you can attend an event at which the vendor is providing a service. Once you are satisfied, make sure you have a document indicating what the company will do for your event. Vendor proposals should include the following elements:

> **Beware!**
> Food and beverages, and the servers that go along with them, are an important part of most special events. In fact, the catering bill often accounts for 40 percent of an event's budget. So pay special attention to choosing the caterer. Ask what the company's specialties are. Also ask to sample every item from the event menu before signing the contract. Many event planners join the National Association of Catering Professionals, finding it a terrific avenue for networking and finding reliable catering professionals.

- Complete description of service
- Description of equipment vendor will provide
- Listing of additional services vendor will provide, if any
- Description of costs and payment terms
- Scheduling information
- Proof of insurance, bonding, and other risk-management practices
- List of vendor requirements (water, electricity, etc.)

In addition, make sure these details all appear in the vendor agreement (see Chapter 4).

Negotiating with Vendors

There are some points on which you can negotiate when hiring vendors, especially as your experience and reputation grow. As a general rule, the more often you have worked with vendors, the more leeway you can reasonably expect them to accord you. Consider asking about the following:

- *Payment terms.* Get your required deposit as low as possible. Also, ask about a prepayment (i.e., paying in full before the event) discount.

- *Complimentary sample (e.g., food-tasting).* This point is especially important either when hiring a vendor unknown to you or when you are asking for something outside the vendor's normal style of service.
- *Complimentary extra.* When you provide a lot of business for vendors, they may be persuaded to throw in something at no charge. For example, a florist who provides centerpieces and other floral arrangements for a large event may provide a free bouquet for the guest of honor.

Hiring Professional Help

You will, at times, need to hire professionals for consultations. Although these services sometimes arrive with a rather steep price tag, it is absolutely money well spent. These professionals will help to ensure the success of your event planning business.

Professional consultants with whom event planners may work include:

- *Accountant.* A good accountant will be your single most important outside advisor and will have the greatest impact on the success or failure of your event planning business. You will have to decide if your volume warrants a full-time bookkeeper, an outside accounting service, or merely a year-end accounting and tax-preparation service. Even the smallest unincorporated event planning businesses employ outside public accountants to prepare their financial statements. All planners interviewed for this book told us they have an accountant. Accountants typically charge $75 to $150 per hour.
- *Attorney.* Finding the right lawyer early is critical. Make sure you hire an attorney you can trust and be comfortable with. You may need your lawyer to help ensure that your business is in compliance with licensing and insurance regulations. A lawyer can also check documents before you sign them and help you draft documents like vendor and client agreements. And, of course, an attorney will help resolve any legal problems that may arise. However, do not wait until you have legal difficulties before hiring a lawyer. Attorney's fees range from $100 to $500 per hour.
- *Business consultant.* You may consider hiring a professional to analyze your

Dollar Stretcher

If you plan on doing most of your bookkeeping and are looking primarily for tax help, consider hiring an enrolled agent rather than an accountant. They can be found in the Yellow Pages or through the National Association of Enrolled Agents (www.naea.org).

Choosing a Lawyer

Consider these factors when choosing an attorney:

○ Will the attorney meet with you in person for an initial consultation—rather than a phone consultation?

○ What is the attorney's background and experience? Specialty? Length of time in practice?

○ Does the attorney have other event planners as clients?

○ Will the lawyer or paralegals perform the bulk of the work?

○ Is there a charge for the initial consultation?

○ What is the charge for routine legal work?

○ Will the attorney work on a contingency basis?

○ Is the attorney's website professional and appealing to you?

○ Always check with your state bar association as well (www.abanet.org).

business plan and check your ideas for feasibility. A good consultant can keep you from making costly mistakes.

- *Event planning consultant.* This individual can help you with all stages of planning an event. If you are new to the industry, consider hiring a seasoned planner whose niche does not overlap with yours.

- *Banker.* The right banker can be a tremendous asset to an event planner. Sometimes, in spite of contracts, clients (especially large corporations) do not pay their deposits on time, says Jaclyn Bernstein. Event planners, however, have to pay vendor deposits. This problem can create a financial crunch for you. However, a banker who has a good, long-standing

Smart Tip

Some venues have exclusive contracts with vendors or have a list of preferred vendors. If the venue has no exclusive contract, then decide on the caterer first and ask for referrals to other vendors. Often arrangements run smoother if the vendors frequently work together. Make sure the contract clearly states what permits and other contractors (e.g., waste removal firm) the catering company will be responsible for.

relationship with your company may "float" you the required funds. "You need a good banker in this business," she says.

- *Insurance broker.* Another professional you will rely on is your insurance broker. Get one who will work with you. If you buy several types of insurance from the same company, you should receive a more attractive deal on the package. Deborah Williams gave all her business to a small insurance company and saved well over 50 percent on her liability insurance.

Remember, investigate well and give careful thought to hiring those who will work with you. The time you invest in choosing your employees and other professionals will pay off in the end as you create a solid, smoothly running team for your business.

Once you have your team, it's time to get the word out! Chapter 7 focuses on how to advertise and market your services and how to improve your customer service.

Marketing Your Business

As you develop your business, it is important to market in order to grow your client base. The planners interviewed for this guide offered varied marketing models. Some successful planners rely solely on word-of-mouth promotion, noting that nothing can compare to a referral from a previous client. Others maintain informative websites or offer their client base a weekly e-mail newsletter. As your company grows, you will determine which model works best. The pace at which you would like your company to grow will determine this, in part. Lauren Polastri had relied solely on word-of-mouth marketing as she purposefully developed a small company, a size she chose so she could also be available for her young children. Now she is ready to move to the next level so is planning to place an ad in her local Yellow Pages.

In this chapter we'll provide suggestions to guide you through the process of developing your strategy and help you evaluate the advertising media commonly used in the event planning industry. We'll also look at several other ways you can promote yourself and your new business.

Networking to Business Success

Virtually every planner interviewed for this guide places networking at the top of their list in terms of developing a strong client base.

Developing a SWOT Analysis

Before you begin advertising and marketing in earnest, develop a road map of your marketing plans. This plan should include a SWOT analysis. SWOT stands for:

- ○ *Strengths*. It is always useful to focus on this question: What are the unique and particular strengths of your business? How do these strengths set you apart from the competition?

- ○ *Weaknesses*. Be honest—even if it hurts! What areas of your business are weak? Develop strategies to combat these weaknesses.

- ○ *Opportunities*. As the name implies, these are things that might benefit your company, now or in the future. For instance, perhaps a new convention center is opening in your area. This is an opportunity for you to grow your business.

- ○ *Threats*. List anything that might harm your business. Perhaps a corporate presence is closing its doors and relocating, or a new event planner is hanging out her shingle.

By focusing on these four areas and writing about them, you will help to focus your marketing efforts.

Dr. Joe Goldblatt, CSEP, founding director of the Event Management Program at George Washington University, explains that networking can prove more effective—and almost always less expensive—than traditional print advertising.

Dallas planner David Granger agrees. The problem, he notes, is that customers need to see what you do, and a word ad won't accomplish that. He recommends networking and making friends in the industry. That way, he says, "People know you, trust you. They want honesty and integrity."

Likewise, industry expert and veteran planner John Daly doesn't use traditional advertising. He networks. He's active in industry organizations like National Association of Catering Executives (NACE) and International Special Events Society (ISES).

Networking can help your business in two ways. If people have met you and know what services you offer, they may refer business to you or use your service themselves. Furthermore, networking with hotels, caterers, and so on will give you a chance to meet some of the people whose services you may need as you plan events.

The Ins and Outs of Advertising

Print advertising covers a broad range, from a free—or inexpensive—Yellow Pages advertisement to an ad in a glossy national publication costing tens of thousands of dollars.

Most planners agree that an ad in the Yellow Pages makes good business sense. A line advertisement, simply listing your business name, is often provided free of charge when you connect your phone. You can also opt for a display advertisement. These are the bigger, bordered ads in the Yellow Pages. There is a charge for these. If you do choose a larger ad space, be sure to include your logo. Also, be aware of the publication cycle of your local phone book. If you open your business in June but the directory isn't published until January of the following year, you will need to look elsewhere to promote your business.

You may also want to consider advertising in your local newspaper. Many papers periodically (perhaps quarterly) publish special sections for brides- and grooms-to-be. These are good vehicles for promoting your event planning business if you plan to do any wedding consulting.

Regional magazines can be useful if you plan both corporate and social occasions. Because the market area for this kind of event planner can extend throughout a given county, a magazine focusing on that county can be an excellent one in which to advertise. These magazines can be geared to topics related to your service (e.g., gourmet food, floral design) or aimed at readers in a certain region. An ad in a regional magazine might be a good tool for reaching upscale consumers. A regional business magazine ad would reach prospective corporate clients.

Advertising in national publications will not pay off for most planners since the cost is simply too prohibitive. Instead, target your advertising dollars on the client base closer to your home.

Your Business Card—Small but Mighty

Don't underestimate the power of this small but mighty marketing tool. Even in the computer age, a succinct, professional printed business card is still critical. Consider it a diminutive brochure, especially if you opt for a tri-fold business card. Many planners opt for this business-card format because more information can be included than on a traditional business card, while the card remains small enough to be tucked inside a wallet or purse.

Include the name of your business, contact information (e-mail, phone, fax, and website address, for instance), your name, specialization, your logo, and some testimonials from past clients. Always check with clients before using their testimonials and ask for permission to use both their first and last names. Testimonials signed by John D. or Jane S. just don't have the same impact as those signed with a full name.

Always carry business cards. You might stand behind someone in the grocery store, strike up a conversation, and discover that she is starting to plan a bar mitzvah. This is the perfect opportunity to pass along your business card. Ask vendors with whom you work (florists, caterers, and photographers,

Smart Tip

As you develop strategies for advertising and marketing your company, remember that your company logo must appear on every marketing piece—from your tri-fold business card to the homepage of your website. This helps prospective clients to remember you and your corporate image. If you haven't had a logo designed yet, now is the time!

for instance), if you can leave a stack of business cards in their places of business.

You can buy blank business cards and print your own if you have a high quality printer. But business supply stores print business cards relatively inexpensively. Choose the best stock (paper) you can afford. Likewise, if you are able to print in more than one color, then do so. For many clients, this will be their first impression of you and your business. Make sure it has a professional impact!

The Informative Brochure

Like your business card, a well-designed, professional brochure can help cement your image as a professional planner. Prospective clients will make judgments about your company based on your brochure, so make sure that it is conceived and produced at the highest level possible.

Beware!
If you decide to try direct mail, don't try to use your mailing list more than once. These lists are "seeded" with control names so the list seller will know if you use the list more than once. Also, make sure you acquire your mailing list from a business in a related industry (e.g., party supply shop, costume shop). This strategy will help target those potential clients most likely to use your services. Also, analyze the direct mailings you receive. What works, and what doesn't?

To achieve this, plan on hiring a freelance graphic designer to help you develop this marketing tool. Tri-fold brochures are popular and allow you to include important information about your business. The brochure should include all of the information listed on your tri-fold business card and allow you to expand upon this information, in particular, by adding photographs. The photos should be of successful events you've designed. You may also want to include a photo of yourself. Because this marketing piece is making a critical first impression on prospective clients, consider hiring a professional photographer to help you obtain first-rate photos. And remember, if you use photos of your events taken by a professional photographer, you need permission to use these images in your printed pieces. You may have to be prepared to pay for them, but more likely the photographer will be happy to let you use them if you provide credit and perhaps their contact information on your piece.

Maximize your chances of success by making sure your company brochure matches the type of business you have. All materials should look professional, but if you are marketing to a budget-conscious group, a too-glamorous brochure can send the wrong message—and send potential budget-conscious clients running in the opposite direction.

As with your business cards, leave your brochure with caterers, florists, photographers, and other vendors with whom you've worked. Provide the vendor with a brochure rack (available at Staples and other office supple stores) so your brochures don't end up in a messy stack on the floor somewhere—not professional!

▲

Direct Mail

You may choose to distribute your brochure via direct mail. If you do so, make sure that your mailing list is well chosen. David Granger says that while word of mouth is their most effective advertising, Designs Behind the Scenes uses mailing lists of the organizations they belong to (ISES, MPI, NACE, and the Dallas Convention and Visitors Bureau).

Newsletters

Newsletters, if written in a lively and entertaining fashion, are useful marketing tools. Mail your newsletter to prospective, current, and previous clients, focusing on what is new in your business. Perhaps you have expanded your services or are offering a specially priced package. Keep the articles pithy and useful. Bulleted points are helpful to your client as are break-out boxes. Your clients' time is at a premium, so keep the articles brief.

You may choose to send your newsletter via e-mail, an inexpensive and effective alternative to the slower "snail mail." Be sure your client wants to receive the newsletter via e-mail. You don't want to be accused of sending spam! See Chapter 9 for more on electronic and social media marketing.

Press Releases

Sending press releases is a fantastic and inexpensive method by which to boost your business. Send releases when you have business news to report—perhaps you have changed locations, planned your 1,000th event, or have some other event that is newsworthy. Newspaper and magazine editors need this so-called news "hook," so don't send press releases without news content. Editors won't run these.

A press release should include:

- *Release date.* Unless your release shouldn't be printed right away, write "For Immediate Release" at the top.
- *Contact name.* Include your name, e-mail, and phone number.
- *Headline.* Editors may change your headline, but give them an idea of the release content with a to-the-point, accurate headline.

- *Dateline.* This is the city from which the release originates. So if your business is in Des Moines, then you should write "DES MOINES" in uppercase type. It should be placed as the first word of type before the press release text begins.
- *Text.* This is your news. Make it interesting to the editor so he will run it!

Most magazines and newspapers prefer that press releases be submitted via e-mail so staff does not have to spend time typing in releases sent via regular mail.

Although the editor may not choose to run all your releases, it is still worthwhile to e-mail them off periodically. One reason for this is that the editor may turn to you when she needs a news source for a story on event planning. Or, she may choose to use one of your releases as the framework for a feature story, which is a larger newspaper article.

The Power of Customer Service

Any business owner—or customer, for that matter—knows the one essential ingredient in running a successful business: customer service. You can be hard working and dedicated, construct a flawless business plan, and have a bottomless source of financing, but if you don't keep customers satisfied and coming back, your event planning business will never succeed.

One of the best ways to keep customers coming back is to be constantly on the lookout for new ideas and for ways to improve the service you provide. Toward that goal, consider the following:

- Take a course (or even a series of courses) in event management.
- Invest in an hour (or more) with an industry consultant.
- Attend other events to study how they are produced.
- Attend as many arts-related functions as possible (e.g., arts exhibits, theatrical performances) to gather ideas.
- Join trade organizations (see "Organization's the Key" on page 104).
- Subscribe to at least one professional newsletter or journal.

Bright Idea
Don't immediately dismiss a customer's creative idea as wacky or not doable. Thoroughly investigate all ideas—not only will your customer be impressed that you took her seriously, but she will also be more understanding if you have to tell her it's not a feasible idea if you can back your decision up with some concrete evidence from your research.

Giving Back to Your Community

Besides providing excellent customer service, earning (and keeping) the goodwill of clients and the community is important. Volunteering your company's help in planning charitable events will win you many friends in the community. And you are sure to gain loyal clients if you are willing to do the following:

- *"Go to the wall" for clients.* All the event planners we interviewed mentioned the need to "make it right," at all costs. This could involve anything from a planner's ability to handle last-minute emergencies to

Keep a list of trusted vendors that you can use for events or to whom you can refer clients. *Photo courtesy of SignatureEventsNH.*

a willingness to "throw in" something extra for free, simply because the planner feels the event would be incomplete without it.

- *Offer clients something they can't get elsewhere.* Many planners mentioned the original aspect of the work they do. More and more, clients want the "different" and "unusual."

- *Make clients feel valued.* Many planners mentioned gifts that they give to clients. These can include everything from cookies and other edibles to unusual decorative items to elaborate floral arrangements. Besides giving gifts, however, there are other ways to make sure clients know they are appreciated. A simple note with a personal message to convey thanks, congratulations, or birthday wishes can mean a lot, as can a phone call. Or, consider putting together a small album of photos from your client's event. Some planners also entertain clients for lunch or dinner.

- *Think less in terms of services and more in terms of problem solving.* Says Joyce Barnes-Wolff, "We try to listen to clients' needs and facilitate them within

At Your Service

If you choose to volunteer your planning services, industry consultant Patty Sachs has some advice for you. First, be sure that the events are ones in which you want to specialize. If you want to focus on board meetings, don't volunteer to plan a birthday party—time spent researching balloon types is not going to help you. Also be sure that the events are high-profile, such as a charity ball or a meeting for members of your city's chamber of commerce. These are the types of events that will be attended by people who may become potential clients. Finally, Sachs says, make sure to get credit for your work—have the phrase "Event Planned by Jane Doe, Anytown, State" delicately yet prominently added to all fliers, invitations, and signs promoting the party, as well as all programs or other materials handed out at the event. If a press release regarding the event is mailed to the local newspaper, be sure you and your company are mentioned somewhere in the release. If the client doesn't intend to send out a press release, consider doing so yourself.

Keep in mind that although volunteering involves a lot of work for no obvious monetary gain, the payoff can be big in the long run. The contacts you make through these first few events will expand into a solid base of satisfied clients who can recommend an experienced, proven event planner to their friends, family, and business associates. Remember, many event planners give their initial clients big discounts in the beginning anyway, because they know it's unfair to charge full price for their inexperience.

their budget. When you have budget restrictions, it forces you to become creative."

Building Your Image

Image—the way your company and its services are viewed by the public—is very important. Some event planners, therefore, will direct much of their advertising and promotion dollars toward building a good company image. You will have to decide how much you can afford to spend to establish, improve, and maintain your image. Increased revenues may be able to compensate for this expenditure.

▲

Organization's the Key

There are several large organizations that serve the special events industry. Most entrepreneurs we interviewed belong to ISES (International Special Events Society), NACE (National Association of Catering Executives), and MPI (Meeting Professionals International). Most also belong to their local convention and visitors bureau. Some belong to the Better Business Bureau as well.

The annual Special Event is the largest and highest profile industry trade show. It is put on every January by Primedia Business Magazines & Media Inc., publishers of *Special Events* magazine. This trade show attracts a couple thousand attendees from around the world.

If you are planning small-scale events with a local focus, you can still benefit from attending the national (and international) conferences. In addition, investigate local and regional organizations in your area. Involvement in industry organizations can provide you with ideas, valuable learning experiences, and excellent ways to network and become known in the event planning industry.

Most important by far, however, is what your events say about your business. The quality of the events you produce is the most powerful shaper of your company's image and reputation.

Don't forget that small details also reflect on you and your company. Remember, Goldblatt cautions, "From the selection of vendors to the choice of brochure paper, every decision you make reflects your taste and company image."

Website Essentials

Having a website is simply a must for any serious business these days. It's just part of doing business in the 21st century. And these days, not only do you need to have a website, but the website has to be well thought out and representative of your business in every way, from design to style to the language you use to describe your business. All of that is doubly critical in a service-based business like event planning.

Here are some basic things to keep in mind about a website for your business:

- Websites give you the ability to change content quickly and cheaply, making it easy to keep the information about your business up to date. Printing a brochure does not afford you that ease of change—in order to keep costs down, brochures need to be printed in high numbers, meaning you may still have hundreds left when you want to change something on it.
- Customers can readily get information, or more information, on your business just by looking at your website.
- The entire world is your market—even though much event planning tends to be locally oriented, there is a lot of destination event business you may capture with a website.
- You can track the results of your marketing efforts more easily with website "hits" and questions/orders you get from your site.
- Your business is open 24/7/365.

Setting Up a Website

If you are one of those people who claim to be computer illiterate and are proud of it, get over it now if you are going into business. If you are adept at using a computer and want to design your own website, that's great, especially if it's going to be an information-only site that won't need the complications of taking orders, accepting payment, or other interactive features.

However, no matter who designs your website, you need to be sure it is professional looking. Just like when you are meeting a potential customer in person, you need your website to express your business style and culture. Some event planners are high-tech, dress in the sharpest new couture, know all the latest caterers specializing in Latin fusion cuisine, and tote an iPad that is used like it is simply part of their body. Other planners are more grass roots in style, dress only in natural colors and fabrics, use a pad and paper to take notes, and are on a first-name basis with all the vendors at the local farmers market. Check out all the websites of different products you are familiar with and get a sense of how their site caters to their buyer base. Your website needs to do the same.

Smart Tip

Using a template doesn't mean you need to or should create a cookie-cutter website—creative and changing content will make your site stand on its own.

Tip...

If you don't feel like you can create the right website, consider hiring a professional web design company. The cost is typically not out of reach; you can expect to spend at least $1,000 for a well-designed, simple site. You will also incur monthly charges to have it "hosted"—someone with a large server keeps everything coming and going. Hosting fees (from as little as $30 a month to several hundred, depending on the complexity of your web business) usually include a certain amount of monthly changes. Again, if you are at all computer literate, part of your options are to have the site set up so you can make changes yourself whenever you want.

Before you hire a designer, look at lots of other event planning websites and make sure you can give the designer ideas on what you like and don't like. Your designer will likely provide you with a few options that you can choose from, either in their entirety or plucking bits and pieces from each.

Find web designers by searching online or noticing who designed the sites you like. The designer doesn't have to be local to design your site—everything can be done, well, online!

You can also buy "template" web designs—you fill the details into a basic design. There are many template companies to choose from, such as www.weebly.com, www,]. web.com, www.wordpress.org, or www.baskweb.com, which includes a shopping cart system. You don't have to be a computer programming wiz as they are designed to be put together by anyone with basic computer skills. Some wireless networks offer the ability to create a website through them. GoDaddy and other domain hosting sites also have templates, although they may cost a modest fee to use.

The design of your site should be simple yet comprehensive. By the time your customers have spent a few minutes on your website, they should have a pretty good sense of your business—especially, being a service business, that customer care is top on your priority list. The good news is that an event planning business is unlikely to need complex elements in the business website—unlike retail, a service business site need to be able to accept payment over the website.

Website Must-Haves

As you create your website, these are "must-haves":

- Homepage
- "Contact Us" page
- "About Us" page
- Testimonials from past clients and vendors. Use real names (with permission), not initials, after the quotes, if possible.
- Photos (make sure you have permission from the appropriate owner of the photo to run these, which may be the photographer or the event client)

- Your company's logo should appear on all of the pages of your website

Your Homepage

Your customer will first come to your "homepage" where you will introduce them to your business and tempt them to spend some time on your site browsing other pages—and ultimately be enticed enough to call you to discuss their event.

Your introduction should include a little history about how you got started, but don't tell every detail about every thought you've ever had about the business. This is a chance for customers to feel like they know you, but don't lose them right at the homepage! Customers want to know right off how you are a solution to their need.

Avoid being too clever. The web customer should open to your site and immediately know they got what they are looking for. Be sure your business name and contact information is right there. And be sure pictures of the highest quality showcase what is clearly an event—and that homepage event should be one in an area in which you specialize. If weddings are your specialty, show a happy bride and groom in a setting that clearly showcases an aspect of the wedding a planner would be responsible for—a stunning table setting, for example. If you do weddings but music events are really your specialty, make sure potential customers land on your homepage and see a picture of a music event.

You don't need and don't want to show everything you do right at the start. The web page might take too long to download to your potential customer's computer; today's computer user expects things in seconds, and they might move on to another website before they even see your homepage. Keep the homepage simple but informative.

By all means, do some advertising on this page—something that clearly reminds the potential customer that your business is solving their problem. "If you want to enjoy your special event, let me take care of the details" or some such blurb might make the viewer really think about how you can help them and push them to pick up the phone and call the number that you so clearly provide on the homepage. How often you can change this page depends on what setup your have with your website provider.

Include a menu of items along one edge of your homepage with headings that the customer can click on to get to that section of your site. Think of it like the signs you see overhead in the grocery store or the pharmacy—direct customers to the sections they are interested in. The person who is looking for someone to plan a corporate event is not interested in seeing the stuff about weddings. Make it easy for the website

Beware!
You can consider linking to the web pages of the companies whose products and services you use, which would give customers information about the great companies you put your trust in, but beware of leading customers away from your site—they may not come back.

visitor to find what is particularly relevant to them.

Drilling Down

Each time the viewer clicks a button on your website they get further into your site. This can be accomplished in two ways—one is with a "pop-up window" where, when they click on a category, the new section pops up over the main page, and when they are finished browsing and close it out, they get brought back to the page they started from. The other "drills" them further and further into your site. Drilling down like this is a common way that websites are set up, but it can get frustrating to your customer if they can't easily get back to a point where they saw something they wanted to look at further. One way to help this is to always have a "home" button on every page—all they have to do is click "home" to get them back to the beginning and find their way forward again from there. It's like having Dorothy's ruby red slippers on your site at all times—only unlike for poor Dorothy, make sure it's clear how easy it is to get home.

The Rest of the Site

Your homepage is one of the most important parts of your website. If you don't capture your visitors at the homepage, they are unlikely to go any further than that. But if your homepage does what it needs to do, they will move to the next levels of your site.

You might include a "button" for each type of event you do or for each service you provide. The homepage for Stargazers Events in Wisconsin (www.stargazerevents.com) has buttons running down the left side of the page that take visitors to information about Stargazers services, a button detailing items they have available for rent such as disco balls or LED tea lights, a button that goes to a page outlining pricing, and one specifically for pictures of events the company has done. Seacoast Events in Massachusetts (www.seacoastevents.net), on the other hand, also has clickable buttons down the side of their homepage, but they take visitors to information about corporate events, weddings, or private functions as well as some of their specialized services such as

Smart Tip
Always include your business's name, address, and phone number on every page of your website. Once customers have drilled a few pages down into your site, they don't want to have to backtrack all the way back to your homepage just to get your contact information.

Tip...

planning boat charters and disc jockey services. Decide what is best for your business and what you want to promote.

Contacting You from a Website

There was a time when small businesses used websites mainly as marketing pieces—people came to the site to view your products, then called to talk with you directly. With the service business, that is still an important role for the website. However, keep in mind that the busy bride-to-be, for instance, is quite possibly browsing websites at 11:00 at night—she can't call you and speak to you then! Having a contact form on your site can be key for this kind of customer. She can feel like she accomplished something if she comes to your site, decides your style appeals to her, and, instead of jotting down your number and trying to remember to call you the next day when you are open, she can simply fill out the online contact form requesting you to call her during the preferred hours she provides in the form.

And, of course, you need to be sure to call her ASAP during her designated time frame! It's important to give the impression that your website is active, up to date, and a critical part of your business marketing.

Trades

If you already have your own website, you can consider finding appropriate sites with whom you can trade ads or products. For instance, "banner ads" (those mini-business-card-size color ads you find around the edges of a website) are often traded among companies whose products and services complement each other. You can put hyperlinks on your website to other companies that you recommend and ask that they put your link on their site.

But again, be careful not to lead your potential customers away from your site to another that can provide them with what they are looking for. The best way to do this is to have the links open as a window so when the viewer closes that window, your site is still open and waiting.

 Beware!
Few things will make a visitor click away from a website faster than finding outdated information. Keep your website up to date. In fact, a good tool to make it clear to viewers that this is an active website is to have something on the site that requires a date—an archive of press releases, a copyright date that changes at least annually, a link to your blog with current entries are some ways that visitors landing on your site see that it is current.

Marketing Your Website

Once you have created your website, don't keep it a secret! While your website may be in cyberspace, be sure your web address is on every printed piece you create for

Get People Clicking

There's no point in having a website if you don't do what you can to get people to click on it. Here are some tips for attracting visitors, and possibly buyers, to your website:

○ Simply tell all your friends and family and ask them to tell all their friends and family.

○ Do the appropriate search engine registration (some web services will do this for you).

○ Make sure every printed and online piece you send to anyone has your website URL listed prominently.

○ Suggest visitors bookmark your site.

○ Trade web advertising with other websites.

○ Create contests with giveaways.

○ Change your website content regularly to keep people coming back to see what's new.

○ Join online discussion groups.

○ If you do public speaking, always mention your site.

○ Provide an "expert" column to newspapers and make sure to mention your website.

○ Connect your website to social media links (see Chapter 9).

These are just a few of a long list of ideas for getting people to come to your website in the first place, keep them coming back, and encourage them to tell everyone they know. Click around to websites in the event planning industry or in any category that interests you, see what catches your eye, and get other creative ideas to drive people to your site.

▲

your business—letterhead, business cards, print advertisements, newsletters (print and e-newsletters), radio ads, everything that has to do with your business should announce your web address. Put the address in your answering machine message. Make sure it is on the door of your storefront if you have one so anyone walking by who either doesn't have time to come in or wanders by during your off hours knows they can find you on the internet.

This all is especially important if your web address is considerably different from your business name—which is not recommended but sometimes can't be avoided if your name is already taken as a web domain by another business.

Your Website URL

Your website has to have a unique address, called a URL or "domain name," that will be used on the server it resides on. Using the name of your event planning business is your best choice; if another business is already using the name you've chosen for your business, pick the next closest name.

Domain names must be registered for a minimum of two years, after which you can renew them. The cost to register a name for two years is approximately $70. There are several companies that handle registration; www.GoDaddy.com and www.Domain.com are well known.

Keep 'Em Interested

Once you get visitors checking out your site, there are some ways to keep them there as long as possible. The longer they are there, the more likely they are to look at everything you have to offer.

Be sure they know immediately whose website they have gotten to. Make it easy

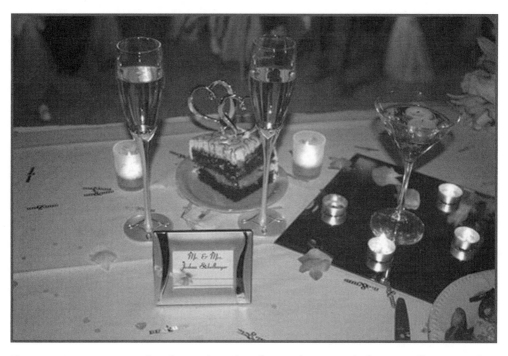

If you are creative, unique details—such as this placecard in a simple frame—will come easily.
Photo courtesy of Stargazer Events.

for them to contact you by having a "contact us" button that makes it simple for them to send you a message.

Keep your website fun and changing. Do contests, include puzzles, add whatever you can for fun interaction, but always connect it to your business.

Many of the planners interviewed use their websites to reach national and international client bases. Says event planner Jaclyn Bernstein, "Websites are great for showing what your company does." However, she cautions that websites can't show everything, and that few clients will hire a planner based solely on a website.

Choosing a Web Host

You must select a service to host your website. Examples of well-known web hosts include Microsoft Network, GoDaddy, and Prodigy, but there are many, many smaller hosts available.

Before choosing a web host, ask these questions:

- How often does the site go down?

- How long does it take to fix the site when it goes down?
- What is its customer support system?
- How many incoming lines does the server have?
- What is the server's experience with high-traffic sites?
- How big is the server?

The price of web fame starts as low as $14.95 per month. Some of the hosts will also allow you to register your domain at the same time.

Beware!

A brief word on ethics: Remember, save your promotion efforts for the right place and time. During an event is not the right time for either you or the vendors you have hired to promote your services. This is the client's event, not yours.

The World of Social Media

Social media and electronic delivery of traditional media is taking on new dimensions all the time. From LinkedIn to Facebook, e-newsletters to ConstantContact, tweets to blogs, and everything in between, no business can afford to ignore social media. However, before you dive in, it is also important to think through all the options, decide which work best for

▲

your business and your schedule, and tie them all together to back up each other's message wherever possible.

Traditional Media with a Digital Twist

Much of traditional media—newsletters, for example—are still used prominently in the business world. However, they are now typically generated digitally and transmitted electronically rather than in print on paper by post. Sometimes, depending on your typical customer base and their computer expertise, companies offer their materials both ways and let the customer decide whether to get their news, ads, brochures, or whatever in print or electronically.

E-Newsletters

An e-newsletter is perhaps the most basic way to communicate with clients—it incorporates a standard format that most people are comfortable with (the newsletter)

Netiquette

The dramatic increase in the use of e-mail has meant that there is a need to practice good etiquette when it comes to e-mailing. The last thing you want to do is offend a customer. So follow these guidelines for proper e-mailing:

○ Never use all uppercase letters; it is considered the equivalent of shouting.

○ Spell-check your e-mails. Just because e-mail is quick, it doesn't have to be sloppy. Not a problem when you are e-mailing with friends and family, but not professional when you are engaging potential clients.

○ Be enticing but also give an accurate sense of what your e-mail is about in the subject line.

○ Create a signature for your e-mail so that every e-mail you compose automatically includes your business name, address, phone number, and e-mail address so the recipient can quickly see how to contact you.

○ Keep your messages short and to the point.

---

and integrates it with the digital format that has become part of everyday life (e-mail). Newsletters that are sent via e-mail are a great way for businesses to keep in touch with their customers. An e-mail newsletter is like a little reminder to your customers that you are there and waiting to fulfill their or their friends', families', and associates' needs.

There are two key things to keep in mind about an e-newsletter:

1. *Creating a newsletter is time consuming.* Just because e-newsletters are cheaper to send (no printing, no mailing costs) doesn't mean you don't need to spend time pulling the newsletter content together. Think carefully about whether a newsletter at all is right for your business and whether the time it takes to pull it together will bring you a return of equal value.

2. *Solicit e-newsletter subscribers on your own website, and on the websites of others.* Sending e-newsletters out unsolicited is considered "spam"; spamming is not only illegal but it creates ill will with your potential customers. But once you create a useful, readable, information-packed newsletter that might even contain a coupon or special or even a giveaway, people will readily subscribe.

Press Releases

Press releases, also called "news releases," should be just that—news. If you have a piece of news to send to the media, by all means do it. A new hire, an expansion of your business into a new market segment, relocation, and accolades for you or your business are all news items about your business. News sources love to get press releases via e-mail; attachments are usually fine but you should check with each individual publication you plan to send to and submit accordingly.

Event listings such as a public event you are in charge of planning or an event such as a bridal show that you are creating are not news and should not be sent in a news release format. You can still e-mail event listings but you should find out who the person is on the staff of newspapers and magazines that handles the event listings in your market.

Also go online and plug your event into all the local event sites that are appropriate—there are lots of ways to get your information on the web!

Smart Tip

Keep an archive of your news releases on your website—it's a great way for the casual browser to check out your professionalism. Also, make sure to list your public events on your own site. If you are doing the planning (or any part of it) for the Rolling Stones concert coming to your area this summer, boast about it on your site! Same if you are hosting a bridal show.

Social Media

The rise of "social media" (defined by Wikipedia as "media for social interaction") presents a fantastic opportunity for all small-business owners to meet and engage with targeted audiences full of thousands of potential customers. The cost of entry into this marketing channel is often only your time—however, don't underestimate the cost of your time! If used correctly, participating in social media will help your business grow through powerful word-of-mouth campaigns.

To get started, there are a few things you should set up right away: a Facebook page, a Twitter account, and a YouTube channel. These social media accounts will become useful tools for you to interact with your audience.

Here are eight great tips on using social media to your advantage from Jesse McDougall, author of *Start Your Own Blogging Business* (Entrepreneur Press, 2010) and co-owner of Catalyst Webworks (www.catalystwebworks.com):

1. Before you start any social media outreach, define your target audiences. How old are they? Do the people in your audience tend to be more female than male? What groups, organizations, or associations are they likely to join? It is unlikely you are going to find groups under the category "people having events." Think about the kind of people you market to and want to use your business—then hang out with them.

2. Once your target audiences are defined, locate them online. Search Facebook, YouTube, Twitter, and MySpace for groups, organizations, channels, or discussions that would contain the people you are looking to meet.

3. Use social media search and organizational tools to help you find your audiences. Some sites, like Facebook and YouTube, have great built-in search functions that will help you find your audience. To find your audience on Twitter, try using external sites like Twibes and www.TwittGroups.com.

4. Once you've found your audience on these sites, join their groups and lists so that you can follow the ongoing conversation. Do not jump right in

> **Fun Fact**
>
> A current trend in the wedding industry are photo booths at the reception—great fun for guests during that lag time between the ceremony and the arrival of the couple at the reception and great memories for the couple. You can choose to purchase items such as this to rent to your clients or you can avoid owning and instead have a solid relationship with a photo booth rental company. Promote this on your website and (with permission) showcase an occasional photo strip on your Facebook page.

with a sales pitch! Listen instead. Learn the etiquette and major players. Spend a week or more just following along.

5. After you're familiar with the etiquette and people involved, jump into the conversation when and where appropriate. Do not hide who you are or the company you represent. Become a regular voice in the conversation and offer your friendly expertise to others. Invite people back to your website and social media accounts to see what it is you do and offer.

6. Once you're a regular voice in the conversation, don't be shy about doing a little promotion. Contests, giveaways, and raffles can be great tools for audience interaction and promotion of your products. People will love the chance to play in your contest and will invite friends to join in the fun.

7. As your audience grows, stay creative. Invent new ways to engage your audience and encourage them to invite their friends. Continue to avoid hard sales pitches. People do not forward commercials to their friends. They forward value.

8. Finally, do not try to do everything everywhere. Sometimes it seems there will soon be as many social media platforms as there are websites. To try to maintain a presence on all of them is unsustainable. Focus on the top two or three that have proven to contain the largest number of people in your target audience.

Remember, social media provides you with the opportunity to meet your audience—not sell to your audience. People do not join these social media networks to find marketers. They join and participate for friendly interaction and the value that that interaction adds to their day. Provide that friendly interaction, and you will watch your audience grow.

Blogs

Blogs, a shortened version of "web log," are typically personal and short diary-like entries that touch on a specific topic. Perhaps you went to an event trade show and found out about a great new trend that your corporate clients might want to think about. Or maybe you went to a seminar on champagnes and want to share what you learned.

Like websites, there are templates, mostly free, available to make the blogging process simple—you sign up, create your blog, write your entries, and the template sets up an archive for you. Blogspot, WordPress, and Blogger are a few more popular blog platforms. Some website templates, like Weebly, offer blogging as an option with your website.

You don't have to be a bestselling writer to write your own blog. But if writing really isn't even a distant strong suit for you, consider hiring a writer to help you with

Entering the Blogosphere

Blogs are essentially online journals or brief newsletters, sometimes with more than one author. You may find blogs useful for networking, brainstorming, and simply commiserating with other event planners. These sites allow for a back-and-forth of ideas and frustrations. Check out www.theparty goddess.com/blog to see what blogs are all about!

it. Create a draft in Word, e-mail it to your writing professional, and he or she can make it zing—and probably edit the grammar and proofread it also. It's worth the small fee that an hour or two a week (or however often you do your blog) will cost. You pay an accountant to make your numbers look right, why not pay a writer to make you sound just right to your target market?

Try to include both pictures and perhaps links to sites with further information in your blog. Don't use it as a strong selling tool. This is your chance to be personal with your clients and potential clients. Give them some good information, and even if they don't use you for their upcoming event, they may use you for their next or they may remember you kindly and tell their friends who are looking for an event planner to check out your blog.

And like websites, no one will know you even have a blog unless you tell the world. Be sure to use phrases in your blog and mark keyword tags that help your blog appear when people search that word or phrase. For example, if you are writing about that champagne seminar, be sure to use the word "champagne" several times in the body of the blog.

You can link your blog to your Facebook and LinkedIn pages as well so your friends and acquaintances on those sites will know when you've posted a new blog entry. It appears with some initial teaser copy, enticing them to click on the link.

Facebook

Facebook is geared toward communicating with your network of friends. However, friends "like" websites that they want to support or really do, in fact, like. So create a Facebook page for your event planning business but use it sparingly for directly promoting too much in the way of business.

Postings to your Facebook wall might include some fun tidbits you learned about a new wedding venue in the region or some behind-the-scenes anecdotes from that

Rolling Stones concert you are coordinating (be discreet and, however, and do this only with permission; Keith Richards may have "told all" in his recent autobiography, but that doesn't mean it's OK for you to tell all about his behind-stage antics you may have witnessed during rehearsal . . .).

Check out the Facebook pages of other event planning businesses and other service businesses that you use and admire to see how they are using Facebook to their advantage.

LinkedIn

LinkedIn is thought of as the Facebook of the business world. The general advice is to make your LinkedIn page more formal than a Facebook page might be. This is where people might go to see your resume, client list, a "serious" picture of you (i.e., a formal headshot, not the picture of your cuddling on the couch with your three dogs).

LinkedIn is almost definitely going to be the more likely place your planning business is exposed to the corporate world. However, no one can see more than the most basic of information about you without you approving making a "connection" with them.

Twitter

A Twitter account for your business may be best used as an extension of a blog. You can send quick messages of up to 140 characters, a "tweet," to your subscribers. "Stones concert shaping up to be best ever!" or "Paul McCartney just said 'yes' to special appearance at Stones concert! Better get your ticket now!" or "Just found out about a great new event venue with full-service spa—does your corporate event need planning?" might be messages that promote your service while also offering benefit to the reader.

> **Smart Tip** *Tip...*
> Twitter—whose "tweets" can only be 140 characters or fewer—is a more casual and personal media outlet like a blog and is referred to as a "microblog."

More social media outlets are coming down the pike every week. The important thing to keep in mind is to use the ones that work best for your business. Don't feel like you have to be involved in all of them. And especially don't overwhelm yourself so that you are spending more time keeping up with social media tweets and posts and don't have enough time for your event planning contracts! You're in business to plan events, not post to social media.

Managing Your Finances

In this chapter, you'll find the basic dos and don'ts for managing your business's money. We'll suggest ways to maintain good cash flow. You'll learn how to arrive at an accurate pricing of your services and how to figure the break-even point for your event planning business. We'll also provide a few tax tips.

▲

Financial Statements

How you manage your financial assets may determine whether your business succeeds or fails. Your capital is not merely a collection of money and property, but a powerful business tool deserving your careful attention. Because going into business for yourself is such a risky proposition, this capital should yield a higher rate of return than an ordinary investment would. Making capital work for you requires careful management of your business, especially of your current and future assets.

Financial management is an area many small-business owners neglect. They get so caught up in the day-to-day running of their businesses that they fail to take a good look at where their money goes.

Stat Fact

Event planners need to keep on top of trends when developing events. From going green (creating completely organic and environmentally friendly events) to the trend toward unusual and interesting ethnic foods, event planners do some of their research at their local magazine rack.

Check out which magazine sections are largest and which magazines are thickest. There has been a proliferation of magazines geared toward Generation Y, for instance. This is a market-savvy group event planners can target and develop.

Keeping good records helps generate the financial statements that tell you exactly where you stand and what you need to do next. The key financial statements you need to understand and use regularly are:

- *Profit and loss statement* (also called the P&L or the income statement). This statement illustrates how much your company is making or losing over a designated period—monthly, quarterly, or annually—by subtracting expenses from your revenue to arrive at a net result, which is either a profit or a loss.

- *Balance sheet.* A balance sheet is a table showing your assets, liabilities, and capital at a specific point. A balance sheet is typically generated monthly, quarterly, or annually when the books are closed.

- *Cash flow statement.* This summarizes the operating, investing, and financing activities of your business as they relate to the inflow and outflow of cash. As with the profit and loss statement, a cash flow statement is prepared to reflect a specific accounting period, such as monthly, quarterly, or annually.

You will need to review these reports regularly, at least monthly, so you always know where you stand financially and can quickly move to correct minor difficulties before they become major financial problems.

Paying Your Vendors

Keeping enough money flowing into a business is a universal concern, but the problem can be especially thorny in an industry that requires the payment of vendor and site deposits often months before an event. Planner Lee J. Howard suggests three strategies for maintaining good cash flow:

1. *Start with plenty of cash reserves.* Make sure that the amount you estimated in Chapter 5 for the first six months of operation is realistic.

2. *Take deposits.* Because you must pay vendor and site deposits and also purchase supplies, you should require deposits from clients upon signing of contracts. Dallas planners Deborah Williams, Kim Quigley, and David Granger require a minimum 50 percent deposit, with the balance to be paid at the time of the event. The deposit for an event contracted with very little lead time may be closer to 75 percent. "You should never be in the business of financing someone's party," says Quigley. Some event planners require full payment before the event to safeguard their financial interest, finding that once the event is finished the client has less motivation to pay.

3. *Charge enough for your services.* Make a careful assessment of what you need to charge to turn a healthy profit.

> **Smart Tip** *Tip...*
>
> Whenever possible, save money by bartering services with other business owners. You could provide planning help in exchange for brochure printing services or the creation of signage, to name only a couple of examples.

Don't low-ball your estimates just to get the job. You'll end up financially frustrated. Remember that controlling costs is easier than trying to predict what your revenue will be. Small expenses add up. For example, why pay extra to have a postal company pick up your packages if you can take them there yourself? Once you look for additional ways to save money, you'll find them. And Benjamin Franklin was right: "A penny saved is a penny earned."

Pricing Your Services

As planner Lee Howard suggests above, charging enough—but not too much!—for your services is key to ongoing business success. It is important for first-time business owners to, therefore, proceed with caution as they first begin to estimate the cost of holding events.

The goal in pricing a service is to mark up your labor and materials costs sufficiently to cover overhead expenses and generate an acceptable profit.

According to industry expert Dr. Joe Goldblatt, fees are typically determined by three factors:

1. *Market segment served.* Social events have a different fee structure than corporate events. In the social events industry, planners typically receive

> **Beware!**
> Remember that small expenses add up. You may supply doughnuts and coffee at morning meetings with your staff. This is great for morale and helps to keep your team happy, but be sure to include a "doughnut allowance" when you calculate expenses!

a fee for their services, plus a percentage of some or all vendor fees. The two income streams produce enough revenue for a profit. If you were to break down your event planning fee into an hourly charge, a social planner would, according to industry consultant and author Patty Sachs, make anywhere from $12 to $75 per hour, depending on experience, plus vendor commissions. In the corporate events industry, however, planners typically charge a fee for their services, plus a handling charge for each item they contract. For example, a

Every ten guests create the need for a new table and all its pieces, adding exponentially to the cost of an event.

planner buys flowers from a florist, marks them up (usually 15 percent), and charges that amount to the client. Another possibility is a flat fee, or "project fee," often used when the event is large and the corporation wants to be given a "not to exceed" figure. Whichever method is used, Sachs estimates an hourly rate for corporate planners of between $16 and $150, plus vendor commissions. As these hourly figures imply, profit margins are typically greater for corporate events than they are for social ones.

2. *Geographic location.* Fees are higher in the Northeast, for example, than in the Southeast. This difference reflects the variation in cost of living. In addition, areas of the country with well-defined on- and off-seasons, such as the Hamptons in New York or Martha's Vineyard, for example, base their prices partly on the season involved.

3. *Experience and reputation of the event planner.* If you are just starting out in the industry, it is reasonable to charge less for your planning services while you gain expertise. A word of caution, though: don't charge too little just to get the job. Although clients shop around for the best price, a planner who comes in too low with an estimate may be as off-putting as a planner who comes in too high. Your client may question your ability to throw a top-tier event based on the price you have quoted.

How, you may ask, are the above-mentioned fees-for-service calculated? Event planners we interviewed price their fees-for-service (the total cost to the client) using a "cost-plus" method. They contract out the labor, supplies, and materials involved in producing an event and charge their clients about 10 percent to 20 percent of the total cost of the event, with 15 percent being a rough average.

A word of caution concerning this method of pricing. Ideally, the percentage you charge above cost should provide you with a sufficient amount to cover that event's share of your overhead, as well as produce a profit. Overhead comprises all the nonlabor, indirect expenses required to operate your business. In general, overhead will be anywhere between 4 percent and 6 percent of the total price of the event. Your actual overhead expenses may vary

Bright Idea

Another way to make sure your business doesn't suffer from a lack of cash is to sell gift certificates toward your planning services. Satisfied customers might buy them, and they are an excellent way to introduce others to your services. Furthermore, gift certificates are money in the bank because people often wait months before cashing them in. Consider, too, if you live in an area with very specific on- and off-seasons, offering $500 gift certificates during the off-season for $450. In this way, you will still keep money flowing into your business during the off-season.

depending on your own market conditions. Should your overhead expenses be too high, you will have to raise your commission to maintain sufficient profit. By raising your commission, you could become less competitive. It's a good idea to closely control your overhead expenses so they don't become too high relative to the price of the event.

When you consider what percent of the total event to charge a client, examine your role in planning the event. Planner Joyce Barnes-Wolff notes that the rule in the industry is to charge, on average, a commission of between 10 percent and 15 percent, depending on what the event involves. She evaluates the amount of her time and energy spent on the event. "My Rolodex is worth something, but if my role is simply picking up the phone and making calls and showing up for an event, I don't think it rates that kind of coordination fee." But if the event is complicated and creativity is what matters, then 10 percent to 15 percent is "very fair," she says.

Industry markups vary widely, ranging from 100 percent and up. Markup rates depend mostly on overhead costs, but the health of the economy also affects them. In troubled economic times, markups (and therefore profit margins) will be lower.

Maintaining Cash Flow

Along with opening your business with adequate cash reserves, requiring deposits, and charging appropriately for your services, there are several other ways of ensuring good cash flow for your business:

- *Pay your company's bills on time, but do not pay early.* Keep your money in the bank as long as possible. The single exception to this rule applies if you have negotiated vendor discounts for early payment (see Chapter 6). Keep files for bills due in 10 days, 20 days, 30 days, etc. Each Monday, pay the bills due in 10 days. Then, transfer the bills due in 20 days to the bills due in 10 days folder, the bills due in 30 days to the due in 20 days folder, etc. This system of files will ensure that your bills are paid on time—thus obviating any possible late fees—but not too early, which would take money out of interest-bearing accounts of your own.

- *Negotiate the latest possible payment of the balance of vendor bills.* Often vendors will give you 30 days after the event in which to pay, especially if you have a good working relationship with them. This means if you get paid on the day of the event, you have 30 days of "free money" before you have to pay your vendors. And if the client is slow in paying, you have a cushion.

- *Make sure your invoices are clear, accurate, and timely.* Being timely means sending your invoices as soon as you sign a contract or complete an event. The difficulty of collecting an account increases in direct proportion to its age. Always itemize invoices so clients know exactly what they are paying for.

- *Keep inventory and supplies to a minimum.* According to industry expert and author Robin A. Kring, excessive overhead and inventory costs can seriously affect cash flow.

Adding Up the Costs for an Event

As we mentioned in the research section in Chapter 3, you have to know exactly what your clients want and what they can spend to achieve it before you can begin planning an event. Then you estimate how much it will cost to contract for labor and supplies, add your commission to this sum, and present the total fee for services to the client as an estimate. Make sure you have filled out the Event Design Worksheet located in Chapter 3. Those client needs will dictate what particular expenses you (and ultimately the client) will incur for that event. Below are some possible per-event expenses:

- *Site rental.* Depending on the event, site rental fees can be considerable, nonexistent, or anywhere in between. This is an opportunity for you to save money for a client on a tight budget. Perhaps a client wants a scenic and sunny summer barbecue. A site at a public beach can often be reserved for practically nothing while tony beach-side clubs often command premium prices.

- *Vendors.* This category could include a caterer, bartender, decorator, florist, photographer, entertainer, videographer, or any of the vendors discussed in Chapter 6.

- *Supplies.* Any supplies not provided by vendors or by the client will need to be purchased by your company. These items can include anything from food to potted trees to table candles.

- *Equipment rental.* You may need to rent audiovisual or lighting equipment.

- *Licenses and permits.* As mentioned in Chapter 4, some types of events require special permits or licenses (e.g., Fire Marshall's permit or a license to use a musical score).

> **Smart Tip**
>
> As an additional way to beef up your cash flow, consider requiring clients to pay your bill in three installments rather than two. The first is the deposit, the second is a progress payment, and the third is due at the event itself. Note that if you do this, you will still probably want to have clients pay a deposit of close to 50 percent.

- *Transportation and parking.* If the event requires you or your staff to travel or requires the provision of transport for attendees or speakers, there may be significant transportation costs involved. These can include anything from airfare to car mileage and gasoline allowances.

- *Service fees and gratuities.* Hiring temporary help (e.g., servers) for the event can be costly.

- *Speakers' fees.* Conferences and other educational or commemorative events often involve speakers.

- *Publicity and invitations.* Getting the word out can be expensive. A large event may be heavily advertised, but even smaller events might entail the use of fliers. Invitations are also frequently necessary. In this age of e-mail, invitations, especially for corporate events, are often sent via e-mail, a budget-conscious choice.

- *Mailing and shipping.* If you are mailing out invitations or fliers, don't forget this expense. Some event planners even ship flowers.

- *Photocopying and preparation of registration materials.* Any handouts for attendees or photocopying of fliers falls under this category.

- *Research and evaluations.* Depending on the nature of your inquiries and whether clients will benefit from them, you may not want to charge clients for these expenditures.

- *Signage.* Any signs or banners designed for the event should be figured into your per-event expenses. As Cheryl Hagner of Wesleyan University says, don't skimp on this. "Signage is essential to a successful event. There must be good flow and signage helps to create this."

Once you know your client's needs and which of the above expenses you will incur in planning the event, you can prepare an estimate of the event cost and of the fee-for-service. First, find out the going rate by contacting three of each kind of vendor you will need. Do the same for suppliers. Don't forget that price is not everything; consider the quality offered. As the saying goes, "you get what you pay for." So, the inexpensive disc jockey might be the guy to tarnish your event, showing up for a black-tie event in his blue jeans.

> **Tip...**
>
> ## Smart Tip
> Although you should strive for an accurate estimate, you may find that your final total differs from the initial estimate. For this reason, you should make it clear to your clients that your estimate of the total event cost is just that—an estimate. Make sure that this fact is stated clearly in your contract. The contract should also specify that the client is responsible for any additional charges. Ensuring that you do not exceed your estimate by an unreasonable amount is an important part of your responsibility to your client.

Finally, calculate the costs for each category listed (and any others that might arise), add them up, and add a small amount for unforeseen expenses (you be the judge of how much, depending on the size of the event).

When you give an estimate to a client, you may want to present it in the form of an itemized list. Show each vendor or supplier separately, perhaps with a brief description of the services he or she is to provide, and list the price of each service. This strategy is helpful, among other things, for reminding clients that your company will receive only a small fraction of the total fee for services. Add all event expenses together, then figure your commission as a percentage of this event cost.

Suppose you are presenting your estimate for an event that costs $6,945 to produce. Let's also assume that you charge a commission of 15 percent—an industry average. After itemizing the event costs, you would add in your commission in this manner:

$$\text{Event Cost (E): } \$6,945$$
$$\text{Commission (C): (15\% of \$6,945) =}$$
$$.15 \times 6,945 = \$1,042$$

Finally, add the event cost and your commission to produce the fee-for-service (S). This figure represents the final cost to the client.

$$\text{Fee-for-Service (S) = Event Cost + Commission =}$$
$$\$6,945 + \$1,042 = \$7,987$$
$$\text{So the final cost to the client is } \$7,987.$$

Calculating When Your Business Will Break Even

We have cautioned you to make sure you have a substantial amount of operating capital, enough to last until you reach the break-even point. How, you may ask, do you calculate a break-even point for an event planning business? The following is a detailed example of such an analysis:

- *Determine your monthly fixed costs.* Fixed costs (F) are those that do not change, no matter how many events you plan (e.g., rent, utilities). You completed a worksheet of these costs in Chapter 5. For the purpose of this break-even example, let's assume that you have monthly fixed costs of $1,910. So F = $1,910.

- *Determine your variable costs.* Variable costs are the costs of putting on the event you produce (e.g., hiring vendors, renting a site). Variable costs combine to produce the "event cost" (E). In this case, E = $6,945.

- *Figure out the fee-for-service (S).* We just did this in the pricing example. We used an average rate of 15 percent, multiplied it by the event cost (E), and produced a commission (C) of $1,042. We then added the commission to the event cost to produce the fee-for-service. S = $7,987.

- *Now use the break-even equation.* Break-even = F divided by C: In this equation, F = fixed expenses and C = commission. Inputting our data from the example above, we find: Break-even = $1,910 divided by $1,042 = 1.8 events.

Beware!

You must keep records to determine your tax liabilities. Regardless of the type of bookkeeping system you use, your records must be permanent, accurate, and complete, and they must clearly establish income, deductions, credits, employee information, and anything else specified by federal, state, and local regulations. You must keep complete and separate records for each business.

According to this break-even analysis, you will need to plan about two $8,000 events per month to pay all expenses and start making a profit.

You and Your Taxes

Managing your finances includes keeping a careful eye on your tax liabilities. These include:

- *Sales taxes.* Sales taxes are levied by many cities and states at varying rates. Most provide specific exemptions for certain classes of merchandise or particular groups of customers. Service businesses are often exempt altogether. Contact your state and/or local revenue offices for information on the law in your area so you can adapt your bookkeeping to the appropriate requirements. Many of the entrepreneurs we spoke to have resale tax ID numbers for their companies. This number entitles a business to buy merchandise (e.g., flowers) tax-free and charge clients the sales tax.

- *Personal income taxes.* If you are a sole proprietor or partner, you will not receive a salary like an employee. Therefore, no income tax will be withheld from the money you take out of your business for personal use. Instead, you must estimate your personal tax liability and pay it in quarterly installments.

- *Corporate income taxes.* If your business is organized as a corporation, you must pay taxes on all profits.

▲

In addition to paying your own taxes, as a business owner and employer you will be responsible for collecting employee state and federal taxes and remitting them to the proper agencies. If you are a sole proprietor and plan to hire an employee, call the IRS at (800) TAX-FORM or access the information at www.irs.gov. Ask for a copy of Form SS-4. Also call your state tax agency.

If you are like most event planners, you will hire some individuals as independent contractors (e.g., vendors). According to the IRS definition, independent contractors are individuals who perform services for more than one firm, determine how the work is to be done, use their own tools, hire and pay their own employees, and work for a fee rather than a salary. If you hire independent contractors, you have to file an annual information return (Form 1099—Miscellaneous) to report payments totaling $600 or

> ## Smart Tip
> _Tip..._
>
> All withheld income tax is treated as if spread equally over the calendar year, even when a disproportionately large amount is withheld in December. If you are required to make estimated tax payments, you should pay special attention to other techniques that may be beneficial, especially if your income is irregular or seasonal.

Working It Out

Good tax planning not only minimizes your taxes, it also provides more money for your business. As an entrepreneur, you should view tax savings as a potential source of working capital. There are a few important rules to follow in your tax planning:

○ Don't incur an additional expense solely for the sake of getting an extra deduction. This strategy is not cost effective.

○ Immediately deferring taxes allows you to use your money interest-free before paying it to the government. Interest rates may justify deferring taxes, though doing so may cost you more taxes in a later year.

○ If possible, claim income in the most advantageous year. If, as you begin your business, you are employed by someone else and expect to receive a year-end bonus or other additional compensation, you may want to defer receipt until the forthcoming year, especially if you will be in a lower tax bracket at that time (e.g., perhaps quitting your job to devote full time to your business).

more made to any individual in the course of trade or business during the calendar year. If you do not file this form, you will be subject to penalties. Be sure your records list the name, address, and Social Security number of every independent contractor you hired, along with pertinent dates and the amounts paid to each person. Every payment should be supported by an invoice from the contractor. Be warned also that if the IRS feels a worker whom you treated as a contractor should have been treated as an employee, you will be liable for payroll taxes that should have been withheld and paid, plus penalties and interest.

Deducting Expenses

As an event planner, you may be able to deduct for the following types of expenses:

- *Home office.* You can deduct for all normal office expenses plus interest, taxes, insurance, and depreciation on the portion of your home that you use exclusively for business. To deduct, however, you must satisfy the following four usage criteria: exclusive use (the space is not used for anything else), regular use (occasional use doesn't qualify), business use (you must conduct business, see clients, etc., in that space), and administrative use (you must handle administrative tasks at that location). Be aware that the IRS audits a high percentage of taxpayers with home offices.

- *Computers.* A home computer used exclusively for business may qualify for appropriate business deductions or credits.

- *Automobiles.* Depending on which method you use, you may deduct for mileage or for mileage plus depreciation, garage rent, insurance, and repairs, among other expenses.

- *Travel.* You must stay overnight on business to claim deductions on air, bus, or auto fares, hotel bills, and incidentals like dry cleaning and gratuities.

> **Beware!**
> Make sure you do not make a mistake about what is tax-deductible. Penalty rates are high. Check with your accountant to be sure your deductions are legitimate. An IRS audit is not only inconvenient, it could be costly.

- *Entertainment.* You can deduct 50 percent of your expenses, but you must maintain records of the following: amount of expenditure; date of expenditure; name, address and type of entertainment; occupation of the person entertained; reason for entertainment; and the nature of the business discussion that took place (general goodwill is not accepted by the IRS). Rules for deductions change frequently. You can also look online at irs.gov for tax updates.

- *Conferences and seminars.* The cost of the actual seminar is deductible, but deductions are no longer permitted for many of the expenses (e.g., food, lodging) incurred in connection with a conference, convention, or seminar.
- *Dues and subscriptions.* You may deduct these as long as they pertain to your field of business.

With proper management of your company's financial resources, you can greatly increase the probability that your business will succeed.

11

Planner
Profiles

The 11th edition of *Merriam-Webster's Collegiate Dictionary* defines "event" as "something that happens," "a noteworthy happening," and "a social occasion or activity." The generality of these definitions make it clear that myriad ways exist to make a living as an event planner.

But each type of event brings with it unique needs from a planner. The person you will be dealing with is quite different for a corporate event compared to a wedding. Although some characteristics are useful in all event planning—calm and confident come to mind—there are some significant differences that are useful from one type of event to another.

This is where thinking about your own personality and what you like to do best comes into play in a big way. Do you have what it takes to spend day after day providing the assurance an emotional bride needs to feel that her big day is going to be perfect? Are you capable of deflecting the steely resolve of a VP who is determined that their corporate event is going to take place in St. Louis even if hotel rooms are scarce due to the city's 50th anniversary celebration of the building of St. Louis's signature Gateway Arch?

In this chapter, we will go through the main types of event planners and some of the key differences for doing each type of work.

Wedding Planners

The wedding planner is perhaps the most ubiquitous event planning category. According to WeTV Network's wedding report (www.theweddingreport.com), 2.08 million weddings took place in the United States in 2009. That is quite a few. And even if only a third of them used a planner, that still totals 690,000 weddings. And although they surely don't break down this way, that would average out to 14,000 weddings in each of the 50 states. If a wedding planner could manage to do 50 per year, that still leaves room for almost 300 wedding planners per state, or 15,000 total.

And it is unlikely that many wedding planners can do a wedding a week with two weeks off for vacations unless they had a decent-sized staff. Many wedding planners work alone or with one assistant. The point being, there is likely room for yet another wedding planner—maybe it's you.

Besides being able to calm the nerves of the most stressed-out bride—or, as likely, mother of the bride—you will need to

- have a great design eye
- enjoy keeping up with trends in things like colors, themes, and food
- do some exploring, patronizing potential wedding venues to be able to make firsthand recommendations
- work on gaining a network of vendors who you know you can depend on to come through with the best of the best and who also recommend you to their clients

- be incredibly organized
- love regularly researching ideas and vendors

Like most things in business, you will need to prove yourself before you can take on getting hired to organize one of the biggest and most stressful events in a couple's life. A good way to get some experience is to provide planning services for a couple friends. Help them make their wedding day absolutely fabulous and then get them to provide you with some testimonials about how fantastic you were and how their wedding wouldn't have been as smooth without you. Then post those testimonials on your website.

As with many event planning categories, you will need to be OK with working weekends, which is when the vast majority of weddings take place. Most wedding planners are on site for the wedding itself to make sure it all goes as planned, to make any last-minute tweaks, and to troubleshoot when problems arise (which they will!). During the busiest wedding seasons—June and September particularly—this will mean pretty much every weekend.

If your business gets big enough and known enough, you might be able to start getting away with being the point person during all the planning phases, making sure everything is set—rentals are scheduled to be delivered, the cake is getting its finishing touches, the bride's gown alterations are done and the gown fits perfectly—and then hand off the on-site follow-through to a trusted assistant (remember Jennifer Lopez's assistant in the film *The Wedding Planner*?).

These days, being a superb planner of any kind, including weddings, means embracing technology. Buy yourself an iPad and iPhone or whatever technological configuration works for you and learn to use them to the outer reaches of their abilities.

Couples who are hiring wedding planners are likely to have a considerable budget for their wedding. To make them comfortable hiring you, you will need to present a polished, professional image. You don't need to spend a lot on office space, but be sure whatever space you have to meet with prospective clients is well appointed and showcases your good taste and design style. Everything about you needs to reflect professionalism and good taste—from your ad in the local wedding magazine to your business cards to your website to how you dress and what greets the bride-to-be when she opens your office door. If you have albums showcasing events you've planned for couples to browse, make sure pages aren't falling out and photos haven't faded or slipped out of place. Better yet, buy a computer with a large-screen monitor for couples to browse independently when they arrive for your appointment.

Although much of the planning can ultimately be done behind the scenes, it is almost 100 percent certain that your prospective couple will want to meet you personally before they sign a contract with you. When they arrive, not only should they have a few minutes to browse an album, but someone should personally greet them. Offer them coffee that is served in attractive matching mugs. Have treats available, perhaps even something with a personal touch. If you know their favorite color is turquoise, have a plate of turquoise frosted petit fours awaiting them. Or maybe you have already learned that they are into NASCAR or horses and the mugs you serve their coffee in reflect that. Wedding planning is an extremely personal service; you need to make it clear to prospective clients that you are interested in them and know how to cater to them personally.

Fundraising Planners

Specializing as a planner of fundraising events can be great fun. There is a huge range of types of events, from auctions to dog walks to motorcycle rides and everything in between. You can do musical events, food festivals like chili cook-offs and pie-making (and eating!) contests, or simple car washes with proceeds donated to a specific cause. Very innovative fundraising ideas have cropped up, from winter polar swims to kissing booths at a Renaissance Faire to dance-a-thons.

Fundraising often is connected to nonprofit organizations. Many nonprofits are small and do not have the budget to hire a fundraising event coordinator. In that case, you either need to approach only large organizations or you need to work up a way to convince the smaller nonprofits that they can afford to hire you—working for a percentage of the proceeds, for example. The more you can prove that your fundraising events are successful, the more you will be able to convincingly market yourself to a group that doesn't have much spare money.

You need to be extremely creative to succeed as a fundraising event coordinator. And you need to be willing to think through soup to nuts everything about the event. Two keys to successful fundraising events are:

1. Always keep it top in your mind that the event is intended to raise money.
2. Marketing, marketing, marketing.

Most fundraising events require people to be in attendance for the event to make money. It is tough to make much on, say, an auction if there are only six people in the room bidding on objects. Those six people most likely have come with a fixed amount

Beware!
When planning a nonprofit fundraiser, don't forget the organization's mission with every decision you make. For example, offering invasive plant species for sale at an environmental group's fundraiser would likely be a bit counter to their mission. And such a group (and most organizations these days) would expect a recycling bin on premises.

of money they are willing to spend that night or they have a specific object they are interested in. Once they have spent that money or bought that item (or lost the bid to someone else), they are probably going to leave or at least stop bidding. You need plenty of warm bodies in those chairs to continue the bidding.

To market a fundraising event like an auction you need to plan well in advance to collect items for the auction that are enticing to get people there. And you need to let them know in advance about these items so they will not only come but come prepared to bid.

And don't be shy about broadcasting that this is a fundraiser! If it is an auction, encourage people to bid high—the auction is not being done to shop for bargains but to support the organization. For all types of fundraisers, find additional little ways for the event to make money—you don't want to dilute the main event, but if the auction includes a bake sale at the back of the room or selling food to be consumed at the event, it not only can raise a little extra cash but can encourage bidders to hang around instead of leaving for lunch and not coming back.

To succeed as a fundraising event planner, you will need to understand how nonprofit organizations operate, know how to work with executive directors and boards, and keep the organization's mission in mind at all times.

Corporate Planners

Corporate event planning can be a fantastic way to earn a living for a planner. Corporate clients usually have a very specific motivation for their event and they are not ashamed to flaunt it, even more than nonprofit fundraisers. Company financial milestones, significant anniversaries, new product launches, employee annual gatherings are all reasons companies need to hire an event planner.

The bigger the company, the bigger the event is pretty much a rule of thumb. But even small companies might need a planner. Planning a successful event is time consuming; small companies are usually streamlined when it comes to personnel so there simply may not be anyone in house who could take the time to plan a sizeable event.

Planning large corporate events that might bring in hundreds of out-of-town attendees requires careful attention to not only the venue itself, but also things like parking, hotels accommodations, area restaurants, and other facilities, and transportation to and from airports and

Smart Tip

Tip...

To locate potential sites for an event, go to www.meet ingnet.com where you can search event venues around the country.

train stations. To make sure large crowds can be serviced smoothly, safely, and conveniently, you'll need to budget a trip to key venues and get to know them firsthand if you are serious about the world of corporate planning.

Educational Planners

If planning educational meetings is up your alley, this is where working for a company as an event planner may be more feasible than going it on your own. Planning professional development, workshops, and training seminars is possible in many categories, from teachers to electricians to sales of all sorts.

You will need to become familiar with the current technology in learning environments to ensure the presenters have the equipment they need to conduct

If corporate clients are a key aspect of your business, you might consider purchasing a podium with built-in sound system. Otherwise, find a couple places to rent one. *Photo courtesy of SignatureEventsNH.*

the seminar. Depending on how many attendees you need to accommodate, even the smallest cities tend to have at least one conference center site and all the fixings that you need to conduct a high-tech event.

Again, visiting venues is key to understanding what is available and to anticipate any glitches that may (or may not!) arise.

Other Event Planners

Although weddings, corporate events, or educational seminars are perhaps the most common categories for event planners to specialize in, there are a lot of other

▲

event planning possibilities. Some of these are complex enough to be your business focus or they could be adjunct to a focus in one of the more common categories. For example, June and September are the most common months for weddings; during the rest of the year, you can fill in the gaps with other events which may be smaller or, at the very least, a nice break from the emotional intensity of wedding planning.

Music Planners

The music industry is a unique animal. It would be difficult to be successful as an event planner for a music venue without having a great love of music. You may want to specialize in booking rock concerts or operas—that's great if there is enough call in your area for one type of music event. There may be a call for organizing the local musical talent of all kinds in your area, from the harpist who would be perfect for weddings if people just knew she was available to the local band that sells out local venues and is on the verge of becoming nationally known.

No matter, the music world is a tight circuit. You need to climb on board and get to know the right people.

Major Milestones Planners

Golden wedding anniversaries and 50th birthdays are lifetime achievements that are often celebrated with a gala event. While many of these events may be small relative to other event planning jobs you could do, they are typically simpler to plan than, say, a wedding. Come up with a basic plan whose details can be tweaked for any theme (gram and grampa are into birdwatching or Uncle Bill rides a Harley), and you can easily create a memorable event that your clients will recommend to all their friends!

Graduations, Homecomings, and More

Adding some basic planning services for smaller events like graduations, homecomings, wedding showers, baby showers, bar or bat mitzvahs, and many other important events in a family's life can be lucrative. Try coming up with some "packages" for these types of events. The market is unlikely to be willing to pay a large fee for a soup-to-nuts event planning service for a baby shower. However, you could come up with a set price that walks a client through the event planning process and provide checklists and sources for materials. And as an added service and added revenue source, you may have a collection of some rental items for such events.

▲

Profiles

Each of the following event planners focus on a different segment of the event planning market. You'll see that there are a lot of ways to enter the world of event planning.

Amy Piper
Signature Events
Wolfeboro, New Hampshire
www.signatureeventsnh.com

Prior to focusing on event planning, Amy Piper—a child psychology major in college and mother who wanted to stay home to raise her children—started her own jewelry design business. But even in that business, she was always planning events, including an artisans' showcase she called "A Gathering of Friends," which she held in her home every year for eight years.

"The success of the annual showcase was my entry into event planning," she says, "and I really enjoyed planning it each year." When a friend who worked at a local private school needed help coordinating events, Piper volunteered. After years of hearing positive feedback about her creativity and organizational skills, Piper finally decided to start Signature Events, and now, 12 years later, she still loves what she does.

One of the company's first contracts was the role of wedding planner for a local historic property, Castle in the Clouds, which overlooks New Hampshire's largest lake, Lake Winnipesaukee, and is a perfect wedding venue. Signature Events helped to plan more than 40 weddings at the Castle in their first year!

These days, Signature Events mixes it up more. Although weddings are the bulk of her business, Piper has also planned many themed events, corporate events, and special events such as family retreats, bat mitzvahs, fundraisers, and golf tournaments. "I like the variety," she admits. "The corporate work is generally more cut and dry, and not as emotional as weddings and other personal events." And Piper loves the aspect of event planning that is critical to be successful in this job: details. "The more details the better," she says. "I love the online research, the phone calls, and creating the event design all while meeting the goals of the budget." Being on the lake, she has done island events that stretch her detail orientation to the max with everything having to be moved to the site via barge. An in-depth timeline for vendors and a collaborative team effort is essential for the success of any event.

Signature Events is located in an in-demand tourist area on a lake that is populated with many wealthy estates. The area is a destination wedding spot—many people have vacationed there and want to get married amidst the gorgeous backdrop with which they are familiar. Being in a small town in New Hampshire's Lakes Region can present its challenges when it comes to hiring specific vendors for large events—"I'm essentially an hour from everywhere," Piper says. "And while I think that it's important to support local vendors, you have to do what it takes for your client, and that often means going with outside resources found in more populated areas to get what you need."

How did Piper deal with the recent recession? "In the midst of the recession, I had the best year ever," she says. Having a huge event helped. But she didn't shy away from taking on lots of smaller events. "You need to be able to go with the flow," she advises, "which can be hard on people [just getting into the business] who are accustomed to getting a paycheck." Piper suggests getting through tough times by looking at how you can direct your concentration and build on more effective marketing strategies. She chose to start focusing on promoting destination events—and now specializes in unique destination venues where she is the exclusive planner for private property owners who want her to promote their property for weddings and events. Early on, she also recognized the opportunities for planning events outside of the Lakes Region as well and has found that she really enjoys the traveling aspect of her job.

Cheryl Hagner
Director of University Events and Scheduling
Wesleyan University, Connecticut
www.wesleyan.edu/eventscheduling

Cheryl Hagner, from whom we have heard throughout this book, started at Wesleyan University working in the library. During that time, she revived the Friends of the Library nonprofit group, which required her to do some fundraising. When the university's event coordination position came up, she took it.

"It was very challenging," she says, "but it helped that I had been at Wesleyan for five years already." The position got even more challenging in 2007, when the university opened a new space. "The events went up dramatically," Hagner says.

Now with more than 16,000 reservations in a year—yes, that's 16,000!—Hagner needed to implement some serious efficiencies. Although she doesn't plan every event, even scheduling is a big job. They use a searchable web interface that allows the reservation process to be more streamlined. Her department has two full-time event planners, a half dozen student workers, and lots of support people, from A/V technicians to electricians to custodial staff as well as public safety and catering.

Hagner stays abreast of the industry through the Association of Collegiate Event Directors, which is where she learned how each university functions uniquely when it comes to campus events.

Hagner has some tips for event planning professionals that she has learned in this interesting and multifaceted event setting:

- It helps to be very organized and not mind slogging through mounds of details.
- Keep in mind that every event has a different set of constituents; you can't treat them all the same.
- "Try not to have your eyes pop out of your head" when the far-out request, like wanting a parachutist to land in a specific spot on the terrace, comes up. "We try in all good faith [to accommodate]—that's my job."

One of her most challenging events was a conference for enthnomusicologists. They had 1,000 musicians on campus for four days. Four hundred papers were presented. And they required videoconferencing to attendees around the world.

Then there are those things that seem small but end up requiring an extra level of service, like requests for dramatic lighting that require an electrician. Or when presidential candidate Barack Obama was the university's commencement speaker. Can you say metal detectors, bomb-sniffing dogs, and sharp shooters stationed on rooftops? "That's an extreme example," Hagner says, "but whenever an event comes up that provides you with a new challenge—that's fun."

The work may be fun, but it's a demanding job. "I'm not always able to leave work behind when I go home," Hagner admits. "But I've gotten better."

Kym Nason
Nonprofit Fundraiser, Connecticut

Kym Nason stumbled into event planning and focuses on the nonprofit world, she says, trying "to be extremely creative to make sure most of the profits go to the organization."

Nason has a degree in communications and worked in advertising and marketing but found she didn't enjoy the corporate world. She opened a dance studio and founded Connecticut Dancers for Good. She had done some fundraising using auctions and wine tastings and then put on a show for Dancers Respond to AIDS. Her marketing background taught her that it's important to keep broadening your own circle.

"I'm in a small state," Nason says, "and businesses are being hit up for money a lot. Right now I am sticking to [collecting for auctions] things that people need anyway."

Nason has remained very focused and stuck with nonprofit dance-related event planning, even though people have tried to hire her for other things that sound exciting.

"I love bringing all the pieces together," she says. "I like the creative aspects of it—who doesn't wish they had an unlimited budget?"

Erin Kelley
Stargazer Events
Kenosha, Wisconsin
www.stargazerevents.com

Erin Kelley caught the event planning bug from her mom, who was always helping with birthday parties and weddings. In business since February 2010, Kelley started out by doing lots of research, especially about the finance end of things.

"The startup expenses surprised me a little," she says. She finds the most challenging financial aspect is trying to market on a small budget. To that end, she is trying to be sure to make use of the free marketing available through social media outlets.

To promote her business, Kelley has done a number of other things:

- She planned a business event that was a little farther from her home turf than she might normally take on, but the event was such a success the president of the is still talking about it. "I like helping other businesses grow just as much as I like growing my own," she says.

- She promotes doing smaller events, capitalizing on the reality that people often find out too late that they don't get to enjoy the event if they are also the party planner. Baby showers, surprise parties, even after-hours networking parties for businesses are fine with her. She is willing to help clients save money by offering the creative ideas for them to carry out, such as table place cards in tiny ornate picture frames it was her idea, but the client went and bought the frames.

- She did a wedding for free and used the wedding photos and comments for marketing testimonials.

- She hasn't hired any employees, but when bigger events come up, Kelley has a ready collection of friends interested in helping.

- She also loves to do her own events! She hosts a St. Patrick's Day event that is the hot ticket among her friends every March 17th.

▲

As a stay-at-home mom, Kelley is trying to balance increasing the number of events her new business does with not taking on too much. "[Stargazer Events] is small, but it's where my heart is," she says. "I don't want to get so big at the moment that someone else has to take care of my kids."

Scott Marshall,
Seacoast Events
Newburyport, Massachusetts
www.seacoastevents.net

Scott Marshall's Seacoast Events has been in business for more than six years. He had been doing event planning for nonprofits and really enjoyed it.

Before opening his doors, Marshall did a formal business plan and full marketing plan. "It definitely helped," he says. And he has continued to adapt and update the plan.

The business maintains a small office, but meeting with clients is mostly done on the road. Marshall would be lost without his BlackBerry, which he uses to schedule appointments and return e-mails while he's on the road.

Seacoast Events focuses on corporate functions, which represent 65 to 70 percent of the company's business. Marshall's personal favorite is the corporate clambake. "Guests really seem to enjoy themselves with a local meal and summer in New England," he says.

Onward and Upward

This chapter has two topics: failure and success.

Because we want to quickly move on to the more cheerful, optimistic topic, we'll first take a swift pass at ways to avoid failure.

▲

Keep Your Business Healthy

We're guessing that what you've read in earlier chapters has already given you an idea of the potential glitches of event planning. If you want to give yourself a little test, put down this book, make a list of the potential glitches you can think of, and then compare it with ours. (If you feel your test-taking days are over, no problem. Just read on.) Here are some of the pitfalls specific to the event planning industry:

> ## Smart Tip
>
> According to Cheryl Hagner, Director of University Events and Scheduling at Wesleyan University, the most important skill an event planner must possess is the ability to put out fires, both literal and figurative. Hagner's office oversees as many as 16,000 events annually—with that kind of volume, problems can and do arrive. She says, though, that her clients remain satisfied as long as she is able to think creatively and resolve the problem quickly.

- *Misunderstanding your client's requirements.* If your client wants a conservative business meeting and you deliver a Roaring Twenties theme party, you're in trouble. Although this is an extreme example, remember that you need to know all your client's requirements in detail before you can arrange a successful event. As Cheryl Hagner points out, this is a particular skill. "Event planners absolutely have to be good listeners and to hear what is said between the lines," she says.

- *Poor choice of vendors or site.* Do your homework. Contract with reliable, reputable vendors who can meet your client's needs exactly. If your caterer serves a terrible meal, it's the caterer's fault that he or she can't cook. However, you're the one who made the hiring decision, so you'll take the blame. The buck stops with you. Be sure you can count on your vendors. Vet vendors carefully. Wolfeboro, New Hampshire, planner Amy Piper lives in a small town on a lake with a large summer community and high property values, which means she plans some significant events. She draws on vendors far and wide, from locally to metro Boston around 90 miles away, to get exactly what her clients want for their event.

- *Lack of coordination between you and your team.* This is a related pitfall. Make sure you have a cooperative, "well-oiled" team (employees, vendors, and temporary staff) around you, and that everyone understands their respective roles in the production of the event. You know the adage—you're only as good as your weakest link. Avoid weak links! Planner Erin Kelley of Stargazer Events in Wisconsin has intentionally kept her business small as she raises her family, but she can say yes to a large event because she has a ready pool of helpers to call on.

- *Inaccurate estimates.* Your estimates should be as accurate as possible. If events go far over budget, your clients may end up having to pay more money than they can afford. If, on the other hand, you consistently come in at or below your estimates, you will probably have satisfied clients who will gladly recommend you to others. Clients may feel "taken to the cleaners" if you come in substantially higher than you originally estimated. Also, you don't want to regularly eat expenses because you inaccurately estimated costs and can't pass them along to your client—that's a quick way to stop your business in its tracks.

- *Inadequate control of costs.* Take every reasonable opportunity to save. Pay attention to where money goes. Compare costs and choose wisely.

- *Poor cash flow.* In Chapter 10 we discussed ways to avoid this problem. One of the most effective ways to counter this is to require client deposits.

- *Inadequate insurance.* Make sure that you carry enough insurance to protect yourself in case anything goes wrong at an event. The planners that we spoke to carry about $1 million of liability insurance. If you don't have enough of the proper insurance, and if you're involved in a lawsuit, you could end up in bankruptcy.

- *Poor customer service.* Much of what we covered in Chapter 7 can be encapsulated into one piece of advice: Make the event right. This is a golden rule in the event planning industry. Nancy Lavin, a regional vice president of an asset management firm, has hired event planners for hundreds of events, ranging from dinners at big-name steak houses to high-touch events at professional sporting events. For her, the deal breaker is poor service. "I understand if problems arise at big events," she says. Things happen. However, the complete deal breaker is poor service. If my client has to wait, then I am not using that event planner again. That sounds tough, but the people I entertain want to be wowed—impressive location, great attentive staff, awesome food."

So how did you do? Now that you know some of the problems that can undermine an event planning business, be alert for any danger signs. If you react quickly enough, you can prevent financial disaster from striking. Ideally, of course, you will not merely react to threats, but instead anticipate changes, whether in the event planning field itself, in your clients' demands, or in the financial state of your business.

Tip...

Smart Tip

If you feel your business is floundering, don't wait to ask for assistance. The Small Business Association reports that too many small business owners ignore financial red flags and don't look for help until it is too late to save their companies. Check with the SBA (www.sba.gov) for advice and guidance.

When Bad Things Happen to Good Event Planners

Even the best event planners face potholes at some events. One thing you can be sure of is having to troubleshoot a problem—it's the nature of the business. It is important to plan for possible large-impact scenarios such as inclement weather for an outdoor event or security-related emergencies. Before the event, take a few moments to think through "what-ifs" and plan crisis management strategies with your staff.

Elite athletes and performers visualize the ski run or the stand-up routine beforehand. Visualize the event. Of course, they practice as well. You will feel more "practiced" with each event you pull off (that old "experience" thing), but there are things you can do to offset problems.

Make sure you know—and have readily available—the facility's emergency and security procedures. Also make sure personnel trained in CPR and other emergency procedures are present at the event.

Occasionally, in spite of your best efforts and meticulous planning, something goes wrong during an event. At that point, your biggest challenge will be to remain calm in the crisis and to think on your feet—chances are if you are getting into this business, you already are pretty good when the panic button gets pushed. However, if you're imagining disaster lurking around every corner, out of your control and waiting to trip you up, take heart. In fact, much of effective troubleshooting is within your control and consists simply of making adequate preparations. In other words, in many cases good troubleshooting is proactive rather than reactive. Try to anticipate where problems might arise and plan for them. This strategy can be as simple as having backups for resources that are critical to an event's success.

> ## Beware!
> With event planning, you don't have a second chance. If an event goes wrong, you can't tell the client to come back the next night. Keep yourself sane, however, by remembering that every event will need some troubleshooting—it may be as simple as the microphone having a dead battery (but you will have fresh ones in your toolkit) to as dramatic as a hurricane landing two hours before the event happens (any outdoor event you plan should have bad-weather alternate plans!). Some event elements will be beyond your control. Be flexible and ready to think on your feet. Finally, don't be defensive with your client. Be professional and take responsibility. Perhaps you need to negotiate a discount if the event was severely disrupted. Or perhaps you can offer a discount on a future service.

Sometimes good troubleshooting involves persistence and a refusal to give up. Atlanta planner Lee J. Howard tells a story of a power failure in a building during one of his company's events. The building manager, who was responsible for backup power, said it wasn't working either and that there was no way to get help until Monday. "Meanwhile, we had a live band and 200 dancers on the floor," recalls Howard. After examining the possibilities, they decided to try all the electrical outlets close to the stage. One in the men's room worked, and they had amplified music back on within 15 minutes. "Although it was July and there was no AC or power for anything else, the party carried on successfully," he says. "The bottom line is, we took responsibility and didn't give up."

Remember, the best way to deal with unforeseen circumstances you cannot control is to remain as flexible as possible and be willing to try new strategies.

Recipe for Success

Besides being a good troubleshooter, what strategies can you adopt to give your event planning business the best possible chance for success? The planners and industry experts we interviewed provided the following advice.

- *Stay calm*, advises Cheryl Hagner. "It sounds like simple advice, but if event planners are able to stay calm—even when the kitchen has been accidentally set ablaze by the caterer—then your client will feel calm and reassured, too."
- *Create good energy at every event*, says Lauren Polastri. Again, sounds simple, but Polastri points out that "you get what you give. Always try to establish a friendly relationship. It's a much nicer way to do business."
- *Acquire professional training*. Says industry expert Dr. Joe Goldblatt, "The shortest route between exploring and succeeding in this profession is affiliation with a well-known school or university." Industry expert John Daly also recommends formal training. Community colleges and continuing education programs offer courses valuable to event planners.
- *Provide the service you say you will*. Use written contracts and stick to them. "And keep good records," suggests New York planner Jaclyn Bernstein.
- *Concentrate on the type of planning you do best*. "Don't try to do it all," advises industry expert and author Robin A. Kring.
- *Create a reliable team around you*. All planners mentioned the importance of staffing and vendor choices. "You design an event on paper," says Martin Van Keken. "Then you rely on other people."

▲

- *Walk through the event.* Event planner Joyce Barnes-Wolff always does a mental walk-through: "In my mind I'm there. Do I have enough time? Are the press kits there?"

- *Event planning is exciting and dynamic, but it is challenging.* As Susan Meyer puts it, "people gravely underestimate what it takes to throw an event." Keep you mind open to continued education and remember that event planning involves a learning curve. The more events you plan, the more confident and accomplished you will become.

- *"Try to be one step ahead,"* suggests Martin Van Keken. "Getting upset doesn't help," he adds.

- *Expect the unexpected.* Many event planners mentioned this one. "There's always something that will go differently than planned," says Van Keken. Not necessarily wrong, he stresses, but differently. "You've got to be ready for that."

- *Be ready with Plan B.* This is closely related to the last piece of advice. "I never do an outdoor event without a rain plan," says Barnes-Wolff.

- *Make your clients happy.* As we have stated, this is a golden rule in event planning. "In this industry there is no right or wrong except to make the client

An Educational Experience

If you decide to get formal training in special events, there are several avenues you can explore. Consider courses in event management through a program such as the one at George Washington University in Washington, DC. Dr. Joe Goldblatt, founder of the program, says that it offers both a master's degree and a certificate program. Certification requires a minimum of seven courses and takes two years to complete. Courses are offered on campus, in five other cities, and through distance learning (i.e., via the internet). For more information, consult the program's website at gwu.edu.

The International Special Events Society (ISES) Conference for Professional Development (CPD) is a series of professional seminars focusing on the latest trends and developments in the special events industry. Offered through ISES, this conference offers both educational and networking opportunities.

As previously mentioned, The Special Event also offers you a chance to learn as you network. Held annually in January, this prestigious industry trade show is put on by Primedia Business Magazine & Media Inc., which also publishes *Special Events* magazine. For contact information on any of these sources, consult the Appendix.

happy," says David Granger. Doing the work and getting it right is what matters, agrees Bernstein.

Looking Ahead

Developing a strong customer base, paying close attention to clients' needs, finding a niche, and coping with a changing economy are all proven ways to keep a business successful and out of financial difficulty. Remember to periodically ask yourself the following questions:

- Have I carefully analyzed the demand for my services, monitored the marketplace, and adjusted to changing conditions?
- Have I found a niche that provides me with enough events to plan, without involving too wide a range?
- Do I have an accurate and realistic amount of cash reserves?
- Do I have a business plan and mission statement?
- Are my services priced accurately?
- Have I kept my overhead costs to an absolute minimum?
- Have I created a good team, with well-chosen staff and vendors?
- Does my company provide the kind of customer service that keeps clients coming back?
- Do I market my company effectively?

If you answered "yes" to all these questions, congratulations! Your company has an excellent chance of success. If you had any "no" answers, these are the areas that need work. And identifying these areas puts you in a good position to make the corrections that will create a thriving business.

Event planning is a "happy" industry. You have chosen a field that will allow you to create wonderful memories for many people. If you do just that, success will follow. So go out there and have fun!

And celebrate!

Appendix
Event Planning Resources

These listings are suggestions for finding event planning resources, from professional associations to useful books, educational opportunities, recommended magazines and journals, and trend-tracking advice.

These sources, though, are only the beginning. They are by no means the only sources available to you, nor can any claim total authority. Event planning is a volatile field, and businesses tend to move, change, fold, and expand. It's up to you to do your homework. Get out and start asking questions.

Make full use of the internet. Because of the fast-changing nature of the event planning field, the web offers invaluable resources. So let your fingers do the walking, on your computer keyboard, to find additional resources.

Associations

The Center for Association Leadership (ASAE), 1575 I St. NW, Washington, DC 20005-1103, (202) 371-0940, www.asaecenter.org

Convention Industry Council, 1620 I St. NW, Washington, DC 20006, (202) 429-8634, www.conventionindustry.org

▲

Event Planners Association, 860-380-3EPA, www.eventplannersassociation.com

Destination Marketing Association International, 2025 M St. NW, #500, Washington, DC 20036, (202) 296-7888, www.destinationmarketing.org

International Festivals & Events Association, 2601 Eastover Terrace, Boise, ID 83706, (208) 433-0950, www.ifea.com

International Special Events Society, 401 N. Michigan Ave., Chicago, IL 60611, (800) 688-4737, www.ises.com

Meeting Professionals International, 3030 LBJ Fwy., #1700, Dallas, TX 75234, (972) 702-3000, www.mpiweb.org

National Association of Catering Executives, (410) 290-5410, www.nace.net

Professional Convention Management Association, 2301 S. Lake Shore Dr., #1001, Chicago, IL 60616-1419, (312) 423-7262, www.pcma.org

Books

This list is literally the tip of the book iceberg in terms of books that might be useful to you. If your specialization is bar and bat mitzvahs, for instance, you will want to research additional titles applying directly to your specialization. The books listed here are more general in nature.

Your local library is a wonderful resource. Also, be sure to check a book's copyright. A book published in the early 1990s, for instance, will lack relevance with regard to the event planning business of today.

Art of the Event, James Monroe and Robert Kates (New York: John Wiley & Sons, Inc., 2005)

The Business of Event Planning: Behind-the-Scenes Secrets of Successful Special Events, Judy Allen (New York: John Wiley & Sons Inc., 2002)

The Complete Guide to Successful Event Planning, Shannon Kilkenny (Ocala, FL: Atlantic Publishing, 2007)

The Complete Idiot's Guide to Event Planning, Robin Craven and Lynn Johnson Golabowski, (New York, NY: Alpha Books, 2006)

Event Planning Guide: Essential Handbook of Meeting, Conference, and Workshop Success for Charity and Not-for-Profit Organizations, Harry Von Bommel (Nova Scotia, CAN: Media Futures Institute, 2006)

Event Planning: The Ultimate Guide to Successful Meetings, Corporate Events, Fundraising Galas, Conferences, Conventions, Incentives and Other Special Events, Judy Allen (New York: John Wiley & Sons, 2000)

Fab Job Guide to Becoming an Event Planner, Jan Riddell, Carol Palmatier, Peter Gallanis (Fabjob.com, 2006)

Pocket Idiot's Guide to Choosing a Caterer, Phyllis Cambria and Patty Sachs (New York, NY: Alpha Books, 2004)

Special Events: Event Leadership for a New World, Dr. Joe Goldblatt (New York: John Wiley & Sons Inc., 2004)

Educational Opportunities

Alan Shawn Feinstein Graduate School, offers the first MBA concentration in Event Leadership, www.jwu.edu

Convention Industry Council, offers training to become a Certified Meeting Professional, www.conventionindustry.org

The George Washington University International Institute of Tourism Studies, offers both a master's degree and a certificate program in event management, www.gwutourism.org

International Special Events Society, provides certification as a Certified Special Events Professional, www.ises.com

Event Planning Software

There are hundreds of types of event planning software, ranging from inexpensive and basic packages to software developed for planning and managing large-scale conventions and trade shows. This software ranges in price from $100 to thousands of dollars. As your company grows, you will need to determine the types of software you will need.

Check out Meeting Professionals International for a detailed look at the characteristics of more than 170 types of meeting software, www.mpiweb.org.

Industry Experts

John Daly Jr., CSEP, John Daly Inc., www.jdalyinc.com

▲

Dr. Joe Goldblatt, CSEP, Dean, Alan Shawn Feinstein Graduate School, Johnson & Wales University, www.jwu.edu

Patty Sachs, author and presenter (with Phyllis Cambria) of several event planning books, www.partyplansplus.com

Magazines and Publications

This listing primarily includes magazines and journals geared toward those in the event planning trade. Remember, any event planner worth her salt also reads consumer magazines to keep on top of trends. For instance, many event planners mentioned *Martha Stewart Living* as a source for current food, floral, and decorating information.

Eventline, weekly e-newsletter, www.specialevents.com

Event Solutions Magazine, www.event-solutions.com

The Meeting Professional, www.mpiweb.org

Meetings & Conventions, www.meetings-conventions.com

Special Events Magazine, www.specialevents.com

Successful Meetings, www.successfulmeetings.com

Travel Weekly, www.travelweekly.com

Websites of Interest to Event Planners

These are some of our favorite websites. As you surf the internet, you will find your own favorites, as well.

www.alltimefavorites.com (All Time Favorites Inc.), a good site for searching for vendors and getting proposals

www.bizbash.com (BizBash.com), a trendy site, featuring lots of ideas for events

www.conworld.net (Conworld.net), contains, among other things, a list of event planning software

www.dmoz.org (Open Directory Project), the hospitality software section in the business area features a long list of software sites for event planning

www.event-planner.com (Event Planner), provides many useful resources

www.eventplanner.com (EventPlanner.com), more resources

www.eventplanning.net (The Event Planning Network), find suppliers, planning tips, chat and discussion areas, etc.

www.event-plans.com (Event Plans), lists many event planning themes and trends

www.expoworld.net (Sponsored by Las Vegas Convention and Visitors Authority), offers many event sites, publications, directories, and articles

www.ezeventplanner.com (EZEventPlanner), use this site to help you plan your entire event

www.ises.com (International Special Events Society), an association of more than 4,000 special events professionals; website features information on joining ISES, a forum for networking with event planners and others in the special events industry, an online copy of ISES' code of ethics, information on local chapters, and more

www.meetings-conventions.com (Meetings & Conventions Online), contains news and feature stories from the latest issue of *Meetings & Conventions* magazine, an events calendar, directory of previously published articles (which have to be ordered separately), plus links to conventions and visitors bureaus throughout the United States

www.mpiweb.org (Meeting Professionals International), an organization of meeting planners for the corporate market (some of whom are independent planners) supports this website consisting mainly of membership information and benefits; you'll also find a database of MPI suppliers, an online version of its bookstore catalog, and local chapter information

www.seatingarrangement.com (SeatingArrangement), plan your seating using information from this site

www.specialeventsite.com (SpecialEventSite), search for many different types of sites

Successful Event Planners

Empire Force Events Inc., Jaclyn Bernstein, www.empireforce.com

JBW Productions, Joyce Barnes-Wolff, www.jbwProductions.com

Lee J. Howard Entertainment Inc., Lee J. Howard, www.leejhowardentertainment.com

The Other Woman, Lauren Polastri, event planner, caterer, and private chef, www.theotherwomancaterer.com

Glossary

Actualization: an accounting of an event planning business's expenditures (both time and money) in producing an event.

American Society of Association Executives (ASAE): an organization for association executives.

Blog: an online journal or newsletter, usually with more than one author.

Bond: an insurance contract used by service companies as a guarantee that they have the necessary ability and financial backing to meet their obligations.

Break-even point: the point at which your company neither makes nor loses money.

Caterer: a company retained to provide food (and usually beverages, too) for an event.

Chat room: on the internet, an electronic gathering place for people who share special interests, where they brainstorm and exchange ideas and information.

Contingency plan: a written plan that is prepared in advance to address possible emergencies.

Contractor: an individual or a company under contract to provide goods or services.

Convention and visitors bureau: nonprofit organization that provides products and services to planners.

Copyright: a form of protection used to safeguard original literary works, performing arts, sound recordings, and visual arts.

Corporate planner: an individual who plans meetings for companies.

Corporation: a separate legal entity distinct from its owners.

Demographics: the primary characteristics of your target audience, such as age, gender, ethnic background, income level, education level, and home ownership.

Destination management company (DMC): a business that handles entertainment for a group of individuals (often conference or meeting attendees) from out of town.

Doing business as (DBA): a reference to your legal designation once you have selected a business name different from your own and registered it with the local or state government.

Domain name: the address of an internet network.

Evaluation: written feedback about an event from attendees or other parties.

Homepage: the gateway to your internet website.

High-touch: A term referring to events that require a high degree of care and handling.

Indemnification: a legal term meaning one party agrees to protect the other party from liability or damages related to an event.

International Special Events Society (ISES): the largest association for special events professionals.

Invoice: a document that indicates costs for goods or services owed by one individual or company to another.

Liability: the legal responsibility for an act, especially as pertaining to insurance risks.

Limited liability corporation (LLC): a business structure combining the tax structure of a partnership yet protecting the owner from personal liability.

Logo: a symbol used to identify or brand your business.

Markup: the amount added to the cost of goods or services to produce the desired profit.

Meeting professional: an individual who plans and provides services for meetings, conferences, etc.

Meeting Professionals International (MPI): the largest association for meeting professionals.

Microblogging: a combination of blogging and instant messaging, where very short messages are sent to update subscribers about the microblog's topic. Twitter is the most well-known microblog vehicle, limiting the microblogger to 140-character messages.

Newsletter: a marketing piece that offers short, newsy pieces about your business. Newsletters may be sent through regular mail or e-mail.

Partnership: a business owned equally by two or more persons.

Proposal: a document outlining what a business will do for a client and the price at which it will be done.

Relational database: a set of data structured so that information can be accessed across different databases.

Site: the location for an event.

Sole proprietor: a company owned by one person.

Supplier: the individual or company that sells goods or services to another company; term often used synonymously with "vendor."

Target market: the section of the market, or group of people, to whom a company hopes to sell its product.

Telemarketing: Using the phone to generate new sales or leads.

Vendor: the company retained by an event planner to handle one or more aspects of an event; term sometimes used synonymously with "supplier."

Vendor agreement: a legal contract between event planner and vendor.

Venue: a site for an event.

Website: a group of related documents posted on the internet, usually accessed through a homepage.

Index

A

accountants, 83, 91
adaptability, 7
adult education programs, 34
advertising, 97–98, 110. *See also* marketing
agreements, 38, 40, 61–67
air travel, 40
answering machines, 74
art dealers, 89
art directors, 87
Art of Event Design, The (Gardner and Terpening), 89
art students, 89
assets, as financing source, 72
associations, 12–13, 16, 90, 104
attorneys, 91, 92
auto insurance, 59

B

balance sheets, 124
bankers, 92
banks, financing with, 72
Barnes-Wolff, Joyce, 5–6, 28
bartenders, 87
bartering services, 125
benefits, employee, 82

Bernstein, Jaclyn, 5, 9, 28, 53, 78
blogging, 119–120
bonding, 60
bookkeepers, 83, 91
break-even point, 70–71, 131–132
brochures, 99
business cards, 98
business consultants, 91
business expenses worksheet, 72
business planning, 15–24. *See also* financing
    business plans in, 21–24, 73
    finding a niche, 14, 17–19
    mission statements and, 24
    overview, 15
    researching industry, 16–17
    startup expenses and, 19–21
business plans, 21–24, 73
business-related events, 10, 19, 126–127
buying equipment, 73–78

C

calligraphers, 87
cameras, 75
cash flow, 124, 125, 128–129, 151
caterers, 87, 88, 90

catering, 35–36

cellular phones, 74

certificate programs, 17, 154

children's birthday parties, 70

client agreements, 38, 62, 63–64

client requirements, 150

clients, prospective, 13

commercial leases, 54

commissions, 128

communications, 7, 43, 70

community outreach, 102–103

compensation, 86

competition, 13–14

computers, 74, 75, 134

confidence, 6

contact forms, web, 110

contact person, 38–39

continuing adult education programs, 34

contracts, 38, 61–67

coordination checklist, 47–48

copiers, 78

copyrights, 57–58

corporate events, 10, 19, 126–127

corporate income taxes, 132

corporate planners, 141–142

corporations, 56–57

cost-plus method, 127

craft services staff, 83

creativity, 7

credit cards, as financing source, 71–72

customer satisfaction, 45

customer service, 101–103, 151

D

Daly, John, Jr., 5, 19, 97

database software, 76

dba names, 53

decision-making skills, 7

décor, 33–35

decorators, 87

deductible expenses, 55, 134–135

degree programs, 16, 17, 154

designers, 82

desktop computers, 75

desktop publishing software, 76

destination managers, 9

details, attention to, 6

direct mail, 99, 100

doing business as, 53

domain names, 112

drivers, 83

E

earning potential, 8, 126–127

educational planners, 142

educational programs, 16, 17, 34, 154. *See also*
    professional development

e-mail, 75

emergency phone numbers, 37

employee taxes, 132

employees, 81–87

    benefits, 82

    family members as, 85

    hiring, 84–86

    overview, 81–82

    payroll taxes, 132

    training, 87

    types of positions, 82–84

    wages, 86

e-newsletters, 116–117

enrolled agents, 91

entertainment, 37, 88

equipment, 73–78, 80, 129

equity, as financing source, 72

errand runners, 83

estimates, 130, 151

etiquette

    e-mail, 116

    telephone, 55

evaluation procedures, 45–48

event design worksheet, 41–42

event expenses, 129–131

event planners, 137–148

    alternate job titles for, 8

    backgrounds of, 4–5

    earning potential, 8

    educational requirements of, 16

    opportunities for, 138

    overview, 137–138

    profiles of, 144–148

    skills needed, 26, 150

    traits of, 5–8

    types of, 137–143

    work schedules of, 3–4

    workplaces of, 4

event planning, 25–48

    coordination phase, 43–44, 47

    corporate events, 10, 19, 126–127

    defined, 2–3

    design phase, 31–38, 41–42

earning potential in, 8
evaluation phase, 45–48
in foreign countries, 2
lifestyle and, 4, 27
overview, 25–26
planning phase, 38–43, 44–45
research phase, 26–31, 130
roles in, 82–83
site selection, 141
social events, 11, 18, 20, 31
trade associations, 12–13, 16, 90, 104
trends in, 30, 35, 124
types of events, 10–11
event planning consultants, 45, 92
event planning industry, 1–14
    event planning basics, 2–8
    growth in, 8–9
    history of, 2–8
    impact of recession on, 26
    keeping up with trends in, 16
    market research and, 10–14
    markets in, 10–11
    overview, 1–2
executive suites, 54
expenses
    equipment, 73–78, 80, 129
    estimating, 70–71, 72
    event expenses, 129–131
    inventory, 78–80
    operating, 70, 72, 80, 131–132
    overhead, 127–128

F
fabric, 79
Facebook, 118, 120–121
fax machines, 78
fees for service, 125–128, 132
50th anniversaries, 83
financial management, 123–135
    break-even point, 70–71, 131–132
    cash flow and, 128–129
    deductible expenses, 55, 134–135
    event expenses and, 129–131
    financial statements, 124
    overview, 123
    paying vendors, 124
    pricing services, 125–128
    taxes, 131–135
financial statements, 124
financing, 69–80. *See also* business planning

business expenses, estimating, 70–71, 72
business plan and, 21–24, 73
inventory and, 78–80
overview, 69–70
sources of, 71–73
fixed costs, 70, 131
flexibility, 7
floral containers, 79
florists, 87
food choices, 35–36
friends, as financing source, 71
fundraising event planners, 140–141

G
general liability insurance, 59
general partnerships, 56
gift certificates, 127
gifts, 78, 79
giving back, 102–103
gofers, 83
Goldblatt, Joe, 8, 25
golden anniversaries, 83
golf events, 5
Granger, David, 11, 18
graphic artists, 88
gratuities, 130
ground transportation, 40

H
Hagner, Cheryl, 5, 145–146
headsets, phone, 39
hiring, 84–86
historic sites, 33
homebased businesses, 54, 55, 60, 134
Howard, Lee J., 4

I
image, 50–51, 76, 98, 103–104, 139
income, 8, 86, 126–127
income taxes, 55, 132–135
incorporating, 56–57
independent contractors, 133–134. *See also*
    vendors
industry trends, 16
industry-related associations, 12–13, 16, 90, 104
installment payments, 129
insurance, 59–60, 151
insurance brokers, 93
internet service, 75
interviewing applicants, 85–86
inventory, 78–80, 129

investors, 72
invitations, 29, 130
invoicing, 128

J

job descriptions, 83, 87
job offers, 86
job requirements, 83

K

Kelley, Erin, 23, 147–148
kid's birthday parties, 70
kitchen staff, 83

L

laminating machines, 78
laptop computers, 75
legal business entities, 55–57
liability insurance, 59
licenses, 57–59, 129
lighting, 35, 80
limited liability companies (LLC), 56
limousine companies, 40
LinkedIn, 121
linking, 109, 110
locating your business, 53–55, 56, 74
logos, 76, 98. *See also* image

M

mailing lists, 99, 100
mailing/shipping costs, 130
major milestones planners, 143
market analyses, 11–13
market research, 11–14
marketing, 95–104
    advertising, 97–98
    brochures, 99
    business cards, 98
    customer service and, 101–104
    direct mail, 100
    ethics in, 114
    giving back and, 102–103
    image and, 50–51, 76, 98, 103–104, 139
    logos, 76, 98
    networking, 96–97
    newsletters, 100
    overview, 95–96
    press releases, 100–101
    publicity costs, 130
    with social media. *See* social media
        marketing

SWOT analysis and, 96
    with websites. *See* websites
marketing directors, 82
markup, 128
Marshall, Scott, 148
meeting management software, 77
microblogging, 118, 121
mission statements, 24
morale, employee, 88, 126
museums, 87
music planners, 143
music students, 89
MySpace, 118

N

naming your business, 50–53
Nason, Kym, 146–147
negotiating, with vendors, 26, 90–91, 128
netiquette, 116
networking, 16, 96–97
news releases, 100–101, 117
newsletters, 100, 116–117
niche markets, 14, 17–19
nonprofit fundraising, 140–141

O

offer letters, 86
office furniture, 74, 75
office managers, 82
online research, 16
operating expenses, 70, 72, 80
organization checklist, 44–45
organizational abilities, 6
The Other Woman, 4, 52
outdoor sites, 33
overhead, 127–128

P

pagers, 74
parking costs, 130
parking personnel, 88
partnerships, 56
payroll taxes, 132
people skills, 7
performers, 88
permits, 57–59, 129
personal income taxes, 132
phone etiquette, 55
photo booths, 118
photocopiers, 78
photocopying costs, 130

photographers, 88
photographs, 61
Piper, Amy, 144–145
planners. *See* event planners
Polastri, Lauren, 4, 27, 52, 96
position descriptions, 83, 87
press releases, 100–101, 117
pricing services, 125–128
print advertising, 97–98
printers, 75
prioritizing, 53
problem solving, 152–153
professional development
    adult education programs, 34
    conferences/seminars for, 154
    degree/certificate programs, 16, 17, 154
    professional organizations and, 104
    resources for, 101
    tax deductions for, 134–135
    trade shows for, 104, 154
professional organizations, 12–13, 16, 90, 104
profit and loss statements (P&L), 124
promotional gifts, 79
proposals, 37, 60–61
props, 79
prospective clients, 13
public relations representatives, 82
publicity costs, 130
purchasing equipment, 73–78

Q
Quigley, Kim, 11, 54, 82

R
record keeping, 43, 46
recruiting job candidates, 84–85, 86
registering names, 53
registration materials, 130
relatives, as financing source, 71
renting
    equipment, 129
    space, 54
room design software, 77

S
Sachs, Patty, 7, 55
salaries, 86
sales staff, 82
sales taxes, 132
scanners, 78
Seacoast Events, 148

seating configurations, 38
service fees/gratuities, 130
serving requirements, 39
signage, 34, 78, 130
Signature Events, 144–145
site agreements, 62
on-site assistants, 83
site rental, 129
site selection, 32–33, 39
skills, required of event planners, 5–8
Small Business Association, 73, 151
social events, 11, 18, 20, 126
social media, 118–121
social media marketing, 115–121
    blogging and, 119–120
    e-newsletters, 116–117
    Facebook, 120–121
    LinkedIn, 121
    online news releases, 117
    overview, 115–116
    summary, 121
    tips for success in, 118–119
    Twitter, 121
software, 76–77
sole proprietors, 55
speakers' fees, 130
specialization, 17–19
spreadsheet software, 76
Stargazer Events, 147–148
starting up, 49–67
    agreements and, 61–67
    expenses for, 19–21
    insurance, choosing, 59–60, 74
    legal business entities, 55–57
    licenses/permits and, 57–59
    locating your business, 53–55, 74
    naming your business, 50–53
    overview, 49–50
    proposals and, 60–61
    summary, 62
startup checklist, 80
startup costs, 19–21
startup worksheet, 21
success, ensuring, 149–155
    overview, 149
    pitfalls, avoiding, 150–151
    strategies for, 153–155
    troubleshooting and, 152–153
supplies, costs of, 129
surveying guests, 46, 48

SWOT analysis, 96

T

tact, 7
taxes, 55, 132–135
telephone etiquette, 55
thank-you gifts, 78, 79
theme parties, 18
tracking records, 43, 46
tracking systems, 43–45, 46
trade associations, 12–13, 16, 90, 104
trade shows, 104, 154
trademarks, 51, 58
training, 87
traits, of event planners, 5–8
transportation, 40, 88, 130
travel deductions, 134
troubleshooting, 152–153
Twitter, 118, 121
typewriters, 78

U

URLs, 112

V

valet-parking services, 88
variable costs, 131
vehicles, 73–74, 134
vendor agreements, 40, 62, 65–66
vendors, 87–91
    agreements with, 40
    catalogs and brochures of, 79
    choosing, 87–90, 92, 150
    coordinating event with, 43–45, 47
    costs of, 129
    independent contractor laws and, 133–134
    information management and, 77
    licenses/permits and, 57, 59
    negotiating with, 26, 90–91, 128

paying, 124, 128
    researching, 27
    types of, 87–88
venture capital, 72
videographers, 88
virus-detection software, 76
voice mail, 74
volunteering, 7, 16, 102, 103

W

wages, 86
walkie-talkies, 78
web designers, 107
web hosting services, 113–114
websites, 105–114
    ads in, 110
    advantages of, 106
    attracting visitors, 111
    contact forms in, 110
    content, 107–110
    designing, 106–110, 112
    domain names and, 112
    hosting services, 113–114
    links in, 109, 110
    marketing, 111–112
    overview, 105–106
    retaining visitors, 112–113
wedding planning, 97, 118, 138–140
Wesleyan University, 5, 145–146
Williams, Deborah, 11, 54, 82
window dressers, 89
word processing software, 76
workers' compensation insurance, 59

Y

Yellow Pages advertising, 97
YouTube, 118